OFFICIAL BUSINESS
DEVELOPMENT SERIES
for Professionals

NETWORKING SUCCESS

INCLUDING Secret Unfair Advantages

Walter Timoshenko

Edited by Alexandra Timoshenko

ASTER HOUSE PRESS
New York
United States of America

NETWORKING SUCCESS: Official Business Development Series for Professionals: Including Secret Unfair Advantages

ISBN-13: 978-1494782740
ISBN-10: 149478274X

Copyright © 2014 Walter Timoshenko. All rights reserved.

No part of this publication may be reproduced or transmitted in any form or by any means, electronic or mechanical, including photocopying, recording, or any information or content storage and retrieval system, without permission in writing from the author. Although the author/publisher has made every effort to ensure that the information in this publication was correct at press time, the author/publisher does not assume and hereby disclaims any liability to any party for any loss, damage, or disruption caused by errors or omissions, whether such errors or omissions result from negligence, accident, or any other cause. If you won't accept these conditions, please stop reading this book now and return it. The author shall not be liable for any physical, psychological, emotional, financial, or commercial damages, including, but not limited to, special, incidental, consequential or other damages. Our views and rights are the same: You are responsible for your own choices, actions, and results. This report is presented solely for educational and entertainment purposes. Any stories, case studies, and examples contained herein and its characters and entities are fictional. Any likeness to actual persons, either living or dead, is strictly coincidental. The author/publisher is not offering it as legal, accounting or other professional services or consulting advice. While efforts have been used in preparing this book, the author/publisher makes no representations or warranties of any kind and assumes no liabilities of any kind with respect to the accuracy or completeness of the contents and specifically disclaims any implied warranties of merchantability or fitness of use for a particular purpose. The author/publisher shall not be held liable or responsible to any person or entity with respect to any loss or incidental or consequential damages caused, or alleged to have been caused, directly or indirectly, by the information or programs contained herein. No warranty may be created or extended by sales representatives or written sales materials. Every individual is different and the ideas and strategies contained herein may not be suitable for your situation. You should seek the services of a competent professional.

OFFICIAL BUSINESS DEVELOPMENT SERIES

NETWORKING SUCCESS

Dear Reader:

Did you ever attend a networking event only to feel:

- underwhelmed?
- lost?
- uncomfortable?
- bored?
- out of place?
- overwhelmed?
- unsure of what to do to get the most out of your time?

Did you ever wonder what to say? What to talk about? How to follow-up? Or even how to escape from someone?

Are you pretty good at networking and want to pick up some techniques that will take you to the major leagues?

Do you run a firm, department, or group, and want some easy to read and understand information to give to other members that will stack the odds for *your* success and *their* success?

If you answered YES to any of these questions, then this book is for you. It's a quick read full of valuable ideas that you can put into action immediately. More importantly, it is designed to work for *you,* no matter what your level is or what position you hold. Newbies to the most senior members of firms have had equally positive results.

Maybe you network infrequently, and even those few events are painful. You don't look forward to them. Then this book may be exactly what you need to pick up a handful of tips to make those investments of your time much more fruitful and enjoyable.

Even as a seasoned pro, you might just find yourself picking up a valuable tip or two to add to your repertoire. Or this may serve as that refresher or reminder that underscores those things you do so well. In any case, networking events aren't going away any time soon. And the skills you will learn in order to be more effective at networking are equally applicable to any host of business interactions, so your time will be well spent.

Along the way, you'll see how to brand yourself, how to become more memorable, how to follow up more effectively, what to research prior to attending events, when to arrive for maximum impact, why you should NEVER be "fashionably late," what to say and how to say it, how to keep conversations alive, how to use the power of contrast, and so much more!

Try it today and see how easy it is to start seeing networking success!

> **"This book shows you why your network soon equals your net worth and how to grow both of them faster."**
> -Brian Tracy
> Best-selling author, speaker, entrepreneur, and success expert

Thanks for the kind words, Brian!

"Networking Success" highlights some of the key points from intensive business and personal development training sessions and seminars. My goal is to stack the odds for *your* success by teaching you some powerful, yet often overlooked, techniques that work wonders for networkers. Check out the Table of Contents to get more of a feel for what you'll learn.

Maybe you got this book because you are looking to grow and develop your own practice or firm, or you wanted to brush up on your skills, or you attended one of my training sessions and wanted a refresher, or maybe you got it from someone who wants *you* to help *them* grow a practice or a firm.

Whatever the circumstances, if you apply yourself to learning and implementing the simple techniques and strategies contained in this book, you will see your networking efforts gain traction like never before.

Welcome aboard!

Table of Contents

SEVERAL TIPS FOR USING THIS BOOK .... - 9 -
A TALE OF TWO EVENTS .... - 11 -
SIMILAR EVENTS, DIFFERENT RESULTS .... - 12 -
HOW DID I GET SO INTERESTED IN NETWORKING? .... - 14 -
APPLYING ENGINEERING TO NETWORKING .... - 18 -
THE RESULTS PROVED THE HYPOTHESIS .... - 21 -
NETWORKING VS. NOTWORKING .... - 23 -
LET'S DEFINE NETWORKING .... - 26 -
WHAT DO YOU EXPECT? .... - 28 -
YOUR UNDERSTANDING VS. THEIR UNDERSTANDING .... - 30 -
MAKING CONNECTIONS .... - 33 -
IT'S PERSONAL, NOT BUSINESS .... - 35 -
BUILD TRUST FIRST .... - 37 -
SQUASHING "RANDOM ACTS OF LUNCH" .... - 39 -
TRAINING AND PROFESSIONALS .... - 42 -
NOT EVERYONE CAN PUNT .... - 46 -
SECRET UNFAIR ADVANTAGES .... -48-
STAYING HEALTHY .... - 58 -
UNCLUMPING .... - 63 -
TEAMWORK & POWER OF THIRD PARTY ENDORSEMENT ...... - 67 -
SINCERE & NATURAL WINS THE DAY .... - 71 -
PRACTICE MAKES PERFECT .... - 74 -
LISTENING .... - 80 -
THE ONE QUESTION YOU MUST ASK .... - 86 -
KEEP THE CONVERSATION FLOWING .... - 88 -

ESCAPING	- 89 -
ONLY* FOR WOMEN	- 93 -
ELEVATOR SPEECHES OR PITCHES	- 96 -
DON'T LEAD WITH YOUR TITLE	- 98 -
BE MEMORABLE	- 100 -
SOME THOUGHTS ON FOLLOWING-UP MORE EFFECTIVELY	- 107 -
HANDWRITTEN NOTES & THE POWER OF CONTRAST	- 110 -
HOW TO FIND PLACES TO NETWORK	- 114 -
A FEW FINAL HINTS	- 116 -
RESOURCES	- 119 -
SPECIAL THANKS	- 120 -
"MAKING YOUR FIRM A BETTER PLACE THAN YOU FOUND IT".	- 121 -
SOME ADDITIONAL VALUE-ADDED INFORMATION ESPECIALLY FOR PROFESSIONALS	- 127 -
MAKE TIME TO MARKET	- 128 -
HOLLYWOOD PRESENTATION SECRETS	- 130 -
ABOUT THE AUTHOR	- 134 -
A PERSONAL THANK YOU!	- 136 -

> *Sometimes, idealistic people are put off the whole business of networking as something tainted by flattery and the pursuit of selfish advantage. But virtue in obscurity is rewarded only in heaven. To succeed in this world you have to be known to people.*
> —US Supreme Court Justice Sonia Sotomayor

Several tips for using this book

As you go through this book you will learn ways to approach networking in a far more strategic way, using some simple yet very valuable tips and techniques to move you far ahead of your competition. The best part is that you might find that you don't really need to make drastic changes. A pilot once remarked to me that if he was only a few degrees off course on a flight from LA to NYC, over the time of the trip, he could end up in Maine. Similarly, maybe all you need to do to reach your goals is to make all the minor little adjustments that will yield the big results you seek.

Time permitting, it is best to read this book from beginning to end. I intentionally kept it rather short so you could finish it in a few sittings.

If you are in a particular hurry, or if you are scheduled to be at a networking event with minutes to spare, feel free to jump straight to the Secret Unfair Advantages midway in the book. But please don't forget to come back and read this other stuff. It's really important.

You will also notice that I have written this series in a Madison Avenue style designed to feel more like a conversation among friends – not a textbook – nor a collection of pontifications or tedious consultant-speak. So, look forward to the contractions, the sentences ending with prepositions, the one word paragraphs and more…There will be plenty to spare.

What differentiates this book from other networking books?

Networking Success covers the very real and practical techniques that few others mention. While some networking guides devote a lot of space to theory and conjecture, *Networking Success* sticks to actionable tips.

The first half of this book contains examples and introduces concepts as it sets the stage for the second half, which presents the Secret Unfair Advantages to networking. You will quickly learn that although they may seem simple (and maybe you'll not even think they are all that much of a secret), these "secrets" are actually very powerful and profound concepts. Also included are Bonus Value Added Suggestions as well as Suggested Action Steps. Everything is designed so that you'll learn the technical ins and outs of networking success coupled with practical tips you can begin using immediately. "Monday Morning To-Do Lists" are places where you can write down those key points that you want to implement as soon as possible.

Networking Success cuts to the chase, making the time you are investing in this book that much more valuable and productive.

So, without any further ado, what better way to start a networking success discussion than to begin with an instructive story? Here we go.

*Networking is not about just connecting people.
It's about connecting people with people,
people with ideas, and people with opportunities.*
— Michele Jennae

A Tale of Two Events

Not too long ago, several entrepreneurs and I were in search of legal and accounting expertise. The work we needed done would top out easily at over a million dollars in professional fees. After we placed calls to many of our sources and contacts, we decided to attend a business networking event and see what we could find. It was held at a prestigious club in NYC. The large room, complete with dark wood paneling and old paintings, was filled with accountants, lawyers, insurance and bank professionals, entrepreneurs, and others.

The place certainly seemed like it was abuzz with life. At times the chatter was so loud it was hard to hear conversations.

And yet, the next day after we compared notes, none of us had been successful in "connecting" with a professional.

Oh, we certainly had conversations with loads of accountants and lawyers. It was just that nobody stood out. None of the professionals had made a favorable impression.

The common theme was that the professionals attending were too busy blabbing about themselves or too eager to dispense advice without listening much.

Similar impressions

As we chatted, we began to realize that we shared many of the same impressions.

One of the entrepreneurs told me that she felt that the CPA she was speaking to was "simply too enamored with himself and his tall tales of his accomplishments to give me the time of day. Of the 20 minutes we spent together, he did most of the talking. To top it off, he never asked me what accounting services I was seeking bids on."

The other entrepreneur reported that while he enjoyed speaking to the attorneys he met, "none of them took the time to really listen to my situation. One actually cut me off mid-sentence and started telling me what I would likely have to do."

Hmmmm…

Similar events, different results

Those same two entrepreneurs and I attended a second networking event shortly thereafter. Each of us walked away with good leads on several professionals for each of the projects we were working on.

We all agreed that, for whatever reasons, the professionals at this second networking event were just that – "professionals."

For instance, one entrepreneur said that he was impressed that the accountant he spoke to asked many questions which he felt were "interesting and on target" and that she made him feel that she really was listening to him.

The other entrepreneur added that "the attorney I met was terrific from the get go. He let me tell him my whole story after which he didn't pepper me with solutions. Instead, he told me about some of his clients with similar issues, and how he had helped them. He was also very forthright about some of the things he tried that worked, and some of the things that did not."

Two similar networking events.

Two very different results.

Why?

Pulling a good network together takes effort, sincerity and time.
— Alan Collins

First, how did I get so interested in networking?

As I set out on my career path, I realized that while networking seemed to be an essential piece of the business success pie, the skills necessary to succeed really weren't being taught in any business school or law school, or as part of any accounting curriculum.

So like many beginners, I stumbled around quite a bit. Chased a load of dead ends. Wasted a great deal of time and energy. All the while, trying to discover what exactly would make networking useful.

Yet, once I discovered the true secrets behind successful networking - it truly clicked for me. I then conveyed this knowledge and experience to literally thousands of professionals across the country. And the ideas and techniques clicked for many of them – people who, like you, were facing the same situations you might find yourself facing. But I am getting ahead of myself.

Early impressions

Many of my early networking experiences were filled with groups of pompous people regaling each other with war stories of their successes. Half the stories seemed to be embellished to the point of silliness. The other half were so boring that I wished that they *had* been embellished.

I may have been a newbie, but I wasn't under any false delusions. Like anyone prospecting for gold, I fully expected to have to move a lot of gravel and sand, but these early experiences were borderline ridiculous!

Where were all the real people?

I remember coming back from one particularly useless networking event, thinking that NETworking events were thinly veiled excuses for NOTworking…

A sea of boasters, blowhards, and others

Typical of my early run-ins was one self-proclaimed guru who would run through networking events and amass pockets-full of business cards. He reminded me of a game show contestant who had been handed a shopping bag and told he had 60 seconds to stuff it full of anything and everything that would fit This networking "guru" would chase people by phone and email endlessly trying to get them to give him business. Clearly, there was no rhyme or reason to his antics. When his business, as well as his guru-status, evaporated several years later, no one was surprised. But none of this shed a light on networking success except as a primer on what NOT to do.

Another person I witnessed would repeatedly show off at various events about his recent "intimate" lunch with a certain Federal

Chairman. He boasted and spewed. When we later learned that the "intimate" lunch had included hundreds of other people at a pay-for-play banquet hall, this man's credibility was toast.

There was also this one woman professional who had apparently convinced herself that she needed to be as "tuff as nails" to fit in with the "old boys club" and "get to the top" – at least that is what she would boast to anyone that would listen. Sadly, she was so over the top loud and demanding that even her own co-workers feared her and steered clear. She swung from being overly endearing one minute to highly obnoxious the next, alienating those around her.

And so it went.

Someone out there had to be doing it right. Right?!

After many false starts and lots of false prophets, I realized that there had to be a better way.

Going to the source

I decided to seek out the most successful networkers I could find. Not the self-proclaimed networking gurus. Not the pied pipers of the networking scene. Instead I concentrated on finding genuinely accomplished professionals, and then studied how they networked.

I carefully watched and studied the approaches used by these successful business developers and proven rainmakers.

Eventually, I decided to actually speak to each directly about their techniques and strategies. Hey, they were bringing in the big bucks, so they had to know what they were doing, right?

Yes! They certainly did. But were they willing to share and reveal? Not so much…

Some were downright cagey. Others seemed oblivious.

Then it occurred to me that maybe some truly couldn't quantify what their secret sauce was – maybe it just came very naturally to them. But natural talent or not, they were still all doing a lot of the same things, and getting great results.

> *Becoming well known (at least among your prospects and connections) is the most valuable element in the connection process.*
> — Jeffrey Gitomer

Applying Engineering to Networking

In order to get to the techniques and strategies, I ended up having to observe and pick up on even their most subtle activities. And pick up I did – coming from a family of civil and military engineers, it was second nature for me to try to discover how things mapped out – how they worked.

I began to attempt to distill networking into its basic building blocks and then to chart a strategic approach to discover the steps and secrets that would make it work for me. Not the stuff based on reputation or fame or DNA. I was looking for the stuff that anyone, experienced or not, could put to work.

RESULTS = C + Mi + Fu

Inherently I knew there needed to be both a "connection" (C), coupled with a "memorable interaction" (Mi), plus "follow-up" (Fu) to get results.

But wait! Think about it. A *connection* alone isn't enough, since I might be quite interested in your service or expertise at the moment, but if I don't remember you later on because there was nothing memorable about our interaction, I will move on, especially in the absence of any follow-up.

Ok. Connection. Memorable interaction. Follow-up.

But was there anything else?

To add a real-life component to my research, I frequently accompanied some of the star networkers in the professional services arena and carefully observed what they did, and how they *really* did it.

I analyzed and over-analyzed networking, the nuances, the subtleties – everything I could possibly find and discover – until I was sick of it all.

Stacking the odds for your success

I had been looking for one big secret, one approach or style or methodology that would put it all together.

Then, after one long day and night of successful networking, it hit me – it was simply about stacking the odds for your success.

There was NO one big hidden secret! There NEVER was.

If anything, it was a whole string of the subtlest little secrets ALL STRUNG TOGETHER. And the more I researched, the more I realized that these "secrets" weren't secret at all.

It didn't matter what the event was, who the participants were, or what time of day or year it was. The venue was almost meaningless, too.

ALL that mattered was making sure that you did enough of the seemingly insignificant things that mega-star networkers did to stack the odds for success.

And NO, you wouldn't have to stay late and work harder. Not at all – in fact I was often able to leave before everyone else – simply because I figured out what I now refer to as my *stacking the odds for your success* approach.

The mark of a good conversationalist is not that you can talk a lot. The mark is that you can get others to talk a lot. Thus, good schmoozers are good listeners, not good talkers.
—Guy Kawasaki

The Results Proved the Hypothesis

Once it all fell into place in my mind, I was on my way. Over the years, my *Stacking the Odds for Your Success* approach has directly yielded 4, 5, and 6-figure opportunities for me and people I know. It opened doors and paved the way for a host of fascinating deals and prospects.

I began sharing my approach and the "secrets" I had learned. And it began to work for others, too.

BTW, I only mention all this "success" stuff to underscore my firm belief that if it worked for me – and for others – it can and will work for you as well, if you are willing to put in the effort and commitment necessary to see it through.

Unfortunately, reading alone doesn't make you thin...

Look at all of the many diets and weight loss systems flooding that multi-billion dollar market.

Ever wonder why, even though the health dangers of being overweight are undisputable, so many folks choose behaviors that keep them obese? Why they start diets only to stop them? Lose weight and then pack it back on?

And then did you ever wonder why health club membership and enrollment numbers far outweigh the number of people that actually show up and exercise?

Simply because ultimately few follow through.

Same with this book. If you don't do it and perfect it, if you don't work regularly at *stacking the odds for your success*, if you don't put in the effort and practice, time and time again, it won't work for you.

As the late great comedian and actor John Candy once said, "I know what I have to do if I want to lose weight and stay healthy: eat a proper diet and exercise. **All I've got to do is apply it**."

So let's see what you can do to apply what you learn and stack the odds for YOUR success as a networking professional.

> *You can make more friends in two months by becoming interested in other people than you can in two years by trying to get other people interested in you.*
> — Dale Carnegie

NETworking vs. NOTworking

Networking should be moving your business agenda forward. Unfortunately, many professionals often find that NETworking is NOTworking. And without a plan and a goal, don't be surprised that NETworking is NOTworking – literally.

For those of you who may have recently completed my *Managing and Marketing Your Professional Services Firm* training, the following discussion will be familiar. For everyone else, let me paint the scene.

Imagine that you are the managing partner of your firm (size is unimportant: solo to mid to super-sized). You have decided that business development via networking is key to your success, and to the success of your firm. You definitely want to align yourself, your key people, and your staff.

So how do you start? What steps do you take to stack the odds for success?

Instant Polarization, and no UV Protection

Not much polarizes a bunch of professionals as much as the prospect of "networking." Most either hate it or love it. Anyone in between, undecided, or on the fence, is just "doin' time."

Networking is like the Sun. It has many positives if you harness them properly. It also has the potential to blind you if you do nothing but sit around and stare at it all day.

For many, networking is a tried and proven way to attract new clients and new business. For others, it is a painful experience second only to public speaking, and it wastes an otherwise good evening. For numerous people in between, networking is a task that they participate in without too much thought that is an occasionally rewarding activity.

The bottom line is whether you're a solo or in charge of hundreds, networking can be one of the best ways to get your message out to the marketplace and find new opportunities, clients, resources, and referral sources.

Might as well make it productive

Since networking it is not going away any time soon, why not make it the most productive and positive experience you can?

But is "networking" limited to official "networking" events? Can't it include chatting it up at a meeting? Striking up a conversation on line at a sports event?

Frankly, networking events can span the gamut from hanging out at a softball game to participating in a high level executive seminar series.

So what exactly is networking?

Think about the last networking event you went to. Was it a holiday party? Was it a CLE class? A charity board meeting? Or maybe a lunch with an old friend or referral source?

Ask a dozen professionals and you'll get quite a few different interpretations of what exactly constitutes a true "networking event."

More confusing could be the results people think that networking events should yield.

But if people really aren't clear on what constitutes a "networking event," how can they possibly agree on what acceptable results are?

Maybe it would make sense at this point to think a little bit about what networking is and isn't.

The richest people in the world look for and build networks. Everyone else looks for work.
—Robert Kiyosaki

Let's define networking

For the purposes of this discussion, let's agree that when you and I talk about "networking," we will include any interaction that you have with other people in a social setting where there is the possibility of expanding your reach, getting your message out there, growing your business, and/or adding to your circle of contacts or sources.

I was thinking about this one day. As lawyers and accountants, we often create the most detailed plans and strategic approaches for our clients. Yet when it comes to investing our own time (and networking takes plenty of time), we often fall short.

I once heard someone describe networking without plans or goals as "random acts of lunch." Well, that's probably not so far from the truth for some. Because if you don't really think about networking, if you don't plan it out, don't set goals, if you simply hope that you will bump into the right people, then you'll risk ending up with lots of activity and little else.

What Tips the Scales?

Interestingly enough, it's often the things you do after the actual formal networking event that make the difference between social chatter and success.

While networking events will often propel you into new and sometimes unexpected areas of opportunity, without structure and strategic follow-up and follow through, not much will happen.

Sometimes when you're at a networking event you can feel the energy all around you. People are excited. They are exchanging ideas and thoughts, interacting, and they are often on their best behavior. It is easy to become lulled into a sense of success, and almost become addicted to the actual networking events themselves. Yet most of the serious work gets done when you get back to your office. It's in the follow-up, follow through, and methodical and structured execution of your next steps that will make the networking that you do successful.

Stumbling Around

I've personally seen quite a few successful professionals who literally stumble through networking events and actually pick up occasional business, simply because they are seen. They might reconnect with old referral sources here and there, and establish a few new relationships. Imagine how much more successful they could they if they actually had a plan.

This leads us to the next discussion – *expectations*.

> *You were born to win, but to be a winner, you must plan to win, prepare to win, and expect to win.*
> —Zig Ziglar

What do you expect?

At our live events, I take participants through a detailed exercise that reveals the many surprisingly contrasting expectations surrounding networking events and how to profit from each. Without the benefit of a live symposium, let's move to better understand expectations as they pertain to us and those around us.

When it comes to "bosses," managing partners, CEOs, senior managers, and even partners in charge of niches, the expectations for results from other staff participating in networking activities can be off the charts. The other people that make up the mix often have very different goals in mind. And these divergent goals are often at the root of a whole slew of business development misdirection and disappointment.

Undoubtedly, if you're a solo practitioner, your goal is typically "to end up with new business."

If you're in a midsize or larger size firm, especially if you're at the partner level, you may very well be looking for new business as well. You may also expect that the senior and junior managers that you send out will have the same mindset.

If you are the managing partner of a firm, you may lull yourself into the belief that surely all members of the firm, *especially your esteemed partners,* are all pulling in the same direction – that *everyone* understands the importance of growing the firm – that if every single person at the firm brought in just ONE new client a year, that the firm would thrive...

We all want to succeed, and we likely have the highest of expectations for our co-workers, our partners, and ourselves.

But do we really have any idea what "they" are actually thinking??

> *No solution can ever be found by running in three different directions.*
> —Deepak Chopra

Don't assume *your* understanding is *their* understanding

Unless you clearly explain your beliefs and expectations, unless you mentor people, and take them along, don't expect them to suddenly come to the same realization and have the same goals that you do.

I have seen far too many professionals attending networking events and simply killing time.

Many junior and senior managers that I've spoken to initially thought networking was simply going out and meeting people.

While in the most basic sense that's true, that's almost like thinking that swimming is only about trying to stay afloat. The reality is that swimming can and should be a lot more than basic survival. And the same holds true for networking.

Mixed messages yield poor results

During my live training, after the group agrees on a definition of "networking," the next step is to define networking "goals."

Talk about mixed messages!

It is almost like playing "broken telephone" to see and hear the wildly varying perceptions that are held about networking and networking goals. From useless and a waste of time to essential and the lifeblood of the firm, I've heard alpha to omega and everything in between.

Quick question: if there is no agreement among firm members regarding what networking is or what its goals should be, are overall poor networking results really a surprise?

Worse yet, many professionals, especially in the middle ranks, are left to figure it out for themselves. As we used to say, "zero support for the ground troops spells tactical disaster no matter how pretty the plan."

Clear communications are key

If any of this sounds familiar, you're not alone. Few firms take the time to effectively and regularly communicate firm-wide goals, let alone what the goals for professional networking should be.

Which brings me to the reason that I brought up this whole discussion: simply doing a better job of communicating what networking is and what its goals are, often is the tipping point that moves professionals into the right direction.

Over the years, I have communicated and reinforced networking expectations and goals via a wide variety of forums including:

- New hire orientations
- Town hall meetings
- Partner meetings

- Staff training
- Memos
- Reviews
- Newsletters
- Website blogs
- Time sheet goals
- Awards and rewards

However you decide to go about doing it, *communicating expectations clearly* is paramount to a successful effort.

Brooklyn is where I primarily developed. I had an opportunity to make records and perform in clubs here and there, and I started networking with the right people in the right places.
—Busta Rhymes

Making Connections

Remember the formula "RESULTS = C + Mi + Fu" ?

Let's take a quick look at C – making Connections.

There are so many ways to make connections. The internet and social media have infinitely expanded the possibilities. But these are simply conveyance methods and platforms.

These new electronic ways to connect, as well as the old ways, all still adhere to the *universal rules for connecting* – a need for feeling and caring and …trust.

Trust!

To truly connect, two people need to feel something for each other. They need to care about each other, even if only a little tiny bit. They also need to feel comfortable with each other. Maybe even be inexplicably drawn to each other. Then, as they interact, and find out that they share some similar experiences or knowledge or interests or whatever, they start to connect and bond. And maybe even trust each other a bit.

I have seen people connect/bond over almost any common or shared interest or experience including a love of dogs, motorcycles, art, kids, poker, schools, golf, natural disasters, food, sports teams, cars, quilts, history, charities, summer camps, and even tragedies (some of the people that I was with on Sept. 11th in Manhattan are still among my closest friends – bonds like that are nearly impossible to duplicate, let alone break!).

Did you notice that one thing is glaringly missing from this discussion?

Think!

That's right! We haven't mentioned purely "business" stuff. In fact, I can't remember ever seeing anyone *truly* bonding or connecting over service offerings, niches, or four color glossy brochures.

> *The currency of real networking is **not** greed but generosity.*
> — Keith Ferrazzi

It's personal, NOT business

Effective connections or bonds are usually FIRST built on a much more personal and social level than on a strictly business level.

For instance, if I don't care much about you or know much about you, if you and I haven't connected on some level, even superficially, if I don't have any reason to trust you, then the chances of you selling anything to me are pretty much zero. (Yes, yes, I would buy a lifejacket from just about anyone on the Titanic. But seriously, no connection – no moving forward.)

Sometimes you connect with someone almost instantly. When you do, think about it. Analyze it. You want to do that more often. The more you learn to connect with people, and build trust, the more you will be able to connect and bond, and then move gradually to the next level.

One of the keys to making connections is trust. Another key is caring. I really care about the people I let into my world. I really care about my friends. I really care about my clients. I care about them as people, as business people, and I care about helping them be successful. And they know it. Caring permeates your actions, words, deeds, everything. It defines you. People can tell when you approach a relationship from a position of strength and caring, or if you are only interested in a quick sale.

Finally, there is a lot to be said for *giving first*. In fact, a recent trend among opinion leaders is to recommend that you give out leads and offer to help others before expecting anything in return. During networking events, this approach says you should concentrate on connecting others, finding out how you might be able to help them reach their goals, and even work on facilitating valuable interactions for them.

While I find this method quite sound in theory, I feel that you need to judiciously monitor your efforts so that you don't turn into a "volunteer do-gooder" for others while your personal core business flounders. Open your spigot as often and as strongly as you want – just make sure that you get something meaningful in return often enough to justify your altruism.

> *If people* **like** *you they'll listen to you, but if they* **trust** *you they'll do business with you.*
> — Zig Ziglar

Build trust first

It is for this lack of connecting that so many networking events fall flat. Without a little interaction, without a little bonding, without a little trust, why even consider doing business with people?

I was at one event where a very pushy fellow literally ran around to everyone and anyone he could find, thrust his business card into their hands, and started asking the most invasive questions of people who were pretty much strangers to him.

He was really aggressive and seemed to think that he was owed attention.

When he got push-back, when people started to avoid him, he blamed the networking group, made a truckload of disparaging statements, adding that he was only trying to "do business" and that it was "just business" to be brash and pushy.

Well... what this fellow had overlooked is that no one yet trusted him. Trust, connections, bonding. It's something you can't fake for long (Bernie Madoff being the exception). Most people can see right through it. And without trust, there would be no connection… and nothing else, for that matter.

Connections, bonding, trust

That's a whole lot to think about, but it is accomplishable.

There is no doubt in my mind that if you truly care about the people you interact with, if you approach your networking with a win-win attitude, and take the time to first build a connection, a bond, and trust, that you will be successful in building those relationships that will help you move to the next level.

Lessons from online trust building

On the internet, it is quite common to give away loads of free quality data in a variety of formats (free reports, books, videos, resource guides, webinars, et cetera) in order to establish a certain level of trust and rapport with your intended audience. After the audience has "sampled" you and your output, they are offered a variety of products they need to pay for. By this time, a certain number will gladly do so since they have positive impressions based upon their experiences.

Extrapolating from the success of this online approach, when networking you could make a concerted effort to show the people you meet just how it feels to do business with you. You could carefully design your interactions to let them sample a bit of your "content" so that they become more comfortable with you. And the more they sample and the more comfortable they become, the more trusting your relationship will be.

Big companies are like marching bands. Even if half the band is playing random notes, it still sounds kind of like music. The concealment of failure is built into them.
—Douglas Coupland

Squashing "Random Acts of Lunch"

Simply understanding and acting upon the real reasons for applying structure and science to networking will yield dramatically better results than participating in "random acts of lunch" – you know, those endless lunches with no clear business goal, no purpose beyond food, and no quantifiable results.

Since no one expects every lunch meeting to yield financial windfalls, and since occasionally, you may bounce into a terrific prospect, random acts of lunch are rarely analyzed. But if they were, you may quickly realize that lunching without a plan or a purpose is a waste of your resources. Whether you are responsible for a group, a firm, or are flying solo, you really want to pay attention to how you invest your time and energy.

Don't mistake activity for progress

A flurry of activity makes you feel as through something of value is happening. People are rushing off to events and meetings. Others are at power breakfasts and networking lunches. You will often hear comments such as "He's always out there," or "She's always meeting new people," or "His week is filled with lunches with new faces."

Unfortunately, the outward appearance of a productive meeting and a random act of lunch is often similar. It is hard to detect what is truly getting accomplished until it is way too late. On the surface, professionals are out meeting people and chatting away under the cover of fine dining. The old "Hey, you never know who you might meet" is thrown around as ground cover while much effort is misdirected.

Ultimately, it all boils down to results.

Given enough time and energy, is anything coming from your efforts? Are you making the progress that you need to be making in order to get to your goals?

How a goal filter can help

If you can get your key players all on the same page and in agreement as to a) what networking is, and b) what the goals are, they will be able to better self-govern their own activities and investments of time.

Everyone should be expected to apply this new *goal filter* to any and all future events. Making these self-determinations a part of your culture will free up your organization from" random acts of lunch" and will also let individuals more confidently map out their own networking calendars, empowering them to routinely say "yes" to time well spent, and "no" to time drainers and wasters.

What should I do if I always seem to be compelled to say "yes" to any request to meet

Just say "no!" if it somehow doesn't fit into your goal filter (while remembering to be pleasant).

Psychologists say it takes about a month to break any habit. At first, it will be a bit counter intuitive to those professionals among you who are accustomed to saying "yes" to almost any offer to meet. After all, you want to be polite, and *hey, you never know*.

After implementing your new goal filter, you often find that you have the same number of meetings and interactions, but that they are far more focused and productive – simply because you now weigh every investment of your time against your goals and targets. You find yourself more focused. Lunches are just as enjoyable, except you are making progress toward some part of your master plan.

If *all* you were to get out of this discussion was an ability to weed out "random acts of lunch" and to refocus on those contacts and opportunities that align more closely with *your* expectations and goals – then it would have been well worth it.

> *"The only thing worse than training your employees and having them leave is not training them and having them stay."*
> — Henry Ford

Training and Professionals

In my consulting practice, we recognize that training professionals to manage and market their practices effectively takes expertise and time. Not everyone is at the same level. Not everyone is comfortable. Not everyone has "bought in."

Networking is no different.

People all learn in varying ways and at different speeds.

And nothing works better than real life exercises, mock events, and a host of interactions designed to strip away fear and doubt and replace these feelings with confidence and empowerment. This is especially important for the women I train, since they are often networking at male-dominated events. More on this later in a Bonus Section just for women.

Nothing makes me feel more satisfied than the calls I get from students and others I've mentored who experience the kind of confidence that networking empowerment training brings.

If you have already completed training with me then you know exactly to what I am referring. You probably see this book as a useful reminder of some of the key points you learned.

If we haven't yet met, maybe someday you and I will have the opportunity to work together. I sincerely hope so. I enjoy face to face training and interactions the best. So until then, this book will provide some of my best tips that you can use immediately with the goal of dramatically improving your networking success.

Isn't it better to get live training?

Absolutely. And making the effort and investing the time in starting to learn is always a huge step in the right direction. But "training" can come in so many different sizes and shapes.

Some professionals perform better when they first read about a topic and then experience it live. Others are far better off just practicing the mechanics with other people, learning from immediate feedback and constructive comments.

Many professionals tell me that even a small amount of live training, in a learning environment, complete with interaction and critique, goes a long way in easing their nerves and preparing them for the "real" thing.

Which leads to a crucial point in the development of any firm or practice – the next generation. Training the next generation is critical.

Forgetting those behind us

After several decades in the professional services arena, nothing pains me more than to see the younger generations of professionals stumbling around aimlessly and often without any career guidance while more established professionals do little, if anything, to help them.

That's a big mistake.

Since few, if any, university courses prepare new members of the professional services arena for business building and networking, then at least exposing new members (or even yourself) to these concepts puts you light years ahead of the pack.

Skills development takes time. And we need to make the time to bring ourselves and those around us up to speed. Investing time in bettering ourselves and our people is always the right decision.

It could be as simple as taking them along

It amazes me how often the front echelons seem to miss opportunities to mentor the more junior members of the firm.

While upper management fixates on developing some formal training program in-house or is busy hiring outsiders to work out grand plans to develop staff or to even launch some version of a "leadership" academy, senior professionals should be looking for ways to develop the levels under them. One look at some of the career and company ranking sites and you'll quickly see that while management may say claim that they "develop" staff, many staffers will beg to differ.

It could be just a matter of mindset. Some senior professionals are often set in their ways and rarely think to take a younger professional along on sales calls, prospect calls, presentations, networking events, client meetings, you name it. A cynical observer might begin to wonder if they fear that someone will see "behind the wizard's curtain." Or maybe they feel that the less experienced will get in their way. Could it be that they just don't think about that next generation or future transitioning? Who knows.

Others have seemingly insulated themselves to the point where they are confident that they will be able to coast to their retirement without having to deal with the pain of networking. As they will proudly announce to you and anyone else in earshot, they're way too busy cranking out billable time to do anything else. Still others will claim that the only purpose of staff is to crank out work and hours.

The truth is frequently somewhere in between.

Suffice it to say, taking junior members along to networking events and client meetings helps them grow and serves as a front-line mentoring tool second to none. The financial health and welfare of your practice and firm is the key here. You all need to work together to find the balance and the allocations of time and talent that will get you to the goals you've set.

Forward. March.

When everyone is on the same page and working together, and when the more advanced people are mentoring and assisting newbies, and when you and your comrades are clear on your networking and organizational goals, then weeding out all of those time-wasting "random acts of lunch" becomes so much easier. Instead of chasing that endless supply of "shiny objects," you and your team quickly evaluates your time investments and choose only those networking events that seem most likely to yield good results.

> *Selecting the right person for the right job is the largest part of coaching.*
> —Phil Crosby

Not everyone can punt

As the quarterback of your team, it's your job to figure out which of your players is good at which plays. Not everyone can punt. Sometimes, it might make good business sense to leave certain players alone to crunch out the billable work while encouraging and training others to flourish in more extroverted ways.

Continually evaluate your team to see who might shine in what situations or at what events. Just because someone flopped at a specific event, for instance an electronics industry networking event, doesn't mean that they are bad networkers at all events. See if you can match them to an industry or an interest that sparks them.

Similarly, if you are a solo practitioner, don't give up on networking based on a bad experience. Keep searching for the right formula and mix that will work for your particular situation. Finding a venue that excites or interests you can go a long way to energizing your drive to succeed.

Commuter vs. NASCAR

By the way, you may find yourself thinking that none of this stuff is truly a "secret." Instead, you may find that the "secrets" are chock full of common sense items that are self-evident. Yet they could be very valuable to those who haven't been exposed to them. I guess it all depends on your perspective.

Here is something I learned about perceptions decades ago while racing cars. To people who have never driven a car, your normal driver's license is the stuff of legends. To a NASCAR pro, it's a joke. Again, it's a matter of perspective.

The good news is that regardless of where you are along the spectrum, you are never too young or too old or too experienced or too new to learn something. That's the beauty of knowledge. You can always learn something new. It's up to you.

Along the way, let's work on *stacking the odds for your networking success* by studying and applying some select "secret" unfair advantages.

For those of you lucky enough to have gone through the live sessions, the rest of this book will be a welcome and familiar refresher of key points. For everyone else, I have put together leading "unfair advantages" to networking success for you to benefit from.

While not exhaustive, make no mistake about it – these are the points that I would share with you if I only had a small window of time and wanted you to gain maximum results.

We're on our way!

Secret Unfair Advantages

Life is about timing.
—Carl Lewis

TIMING

"Go Early, Be First"

Here is one of my TOP networking tips ever – Go early, be first!

Many professionals tell me that they find it hard to walk into a crowded room and make sense of the potential opportunities. I can empathize. Instead of an intimate setting, you are thrust into a large room with a ton of people. Everyone seems to know each other.

And then there's you.

Wouldn't it be better to have been there at the start and have been part of the growth?

When you arrive at a networking event a bit early, you often have access to the organizers of the event as well as to any special guests or speakers. You tend to be able to strike up conversations better since the crowds haven't descended yet. And it is a lot less hectic at the beginning. If you are naturally introverted, or tend to be more introspective, then nothing beats showing up early!

"HOST" vs. "GUEST" DYNAMIC

Being early has another solid advantage – this one has to do with group dynamics. When you arrive early and are already in the room as others arrive, then suddenly you become more of a host than a guest.

The whole dynamic of networking can change (for the better) when you are first in the room. As people show up, you are now in the position of welcoming them. You have become part of the "establishment." You are part of the "in crowd" simply since you are already "in" the room.

Use this to your advantage by playing the role of a pseudo-host and welcoming others in.

How you make them feel

It has been said that people may soon forget names and titles and sales speeches. But they are slow to forget how someone made them feel. Further, people remember those that welcomed them and made them feel at home or good about themselves or a situation.

New arrivers are often uncomfortable, so a smile and a friendly gesture are terrific ice-breakers. Look for some neutral common ground – maybe it will be a light hearted comment about the weather, the parking situation, or even the organization hosting the event.

Just keep it matter-of-fact and upbeat, since you don't know who knows whom, or who invited whom, et cetera. At the same time, don't be *overly* friendly or clingy – stay professional and network, network, network.

How early is *early*?

Some of the more analytical people in my live training class have raised timing issues – how early is early?

If you arrive too early you run the risk of getting in the way of last minute preparations. And we all know why you shouldn't arrive late.

So, I feel that "early" is 5 minutes early – and it usually gets you there ahead of the crowd. Use your common sense and adjust as necessary. In the end, timing has to work for you.

Who is going to an event?

Knowing who will be at an event ahead of time allows you to make the most of your time, especially if certain companies of industries of interest to you will be represented.

(By the way, if you haven't learned to research people and topics on the internet, you don't have to admit it to anyone ever. But do something about it *today*. Take a course. Play around a bit online and figure it out. It can make a world of difference.)

Some things to keep in mind while researching guest lists

• Who else will be there?

• Are they the "END GAME" or might they know those I want to meet?

• Who is scheduled to speak or present?

• Whom do I want to meet and why?

Do some digging and find some interesting ways to connect with the people you have identified as "persons of interest."

Keep in mind that you want to-

- Learn more about them, their work, their company, and their interests.

- See if you can come up with a trend affecting their business, and chat with them about it.

- Ask them what the top concerns are for people in their industry.

- Mentions some of the items that you do that may be relevant to their business.

- Don't sell blatantly. It is time to forge relationships.

- Try and connect with them on a personal level based on interests or experiences you may share – schools attended, hobbies, philanthropic pursuits, and the like.

- When discussing business, instead of blabbering like a brochure, instead tell stories, or give examples, which demonstrate how your expertise successfully assisted someone.

ACTION STEPS

• Take a look at your upcoming networking calendar (you do have one, right?) and figure out a plan that will get you to each event a few minutes early so that you are there on time and among the first to arrive.

• Contact each networking event coordinator and ask if there is a guest list available to review prior to the event. Don't overlook the internet. Sometimes, attendees are listed on the organizer's website. If no RSVP list is available, try to see who is sponsoring the event. Maybe some of the sponsors will prove interesting to you.

• Be familiar with who the hosts of the networking event are. Is there anything interesting about them that you can find out prior to the event? Is there some topic you can research that might be of interest to them?

MONDAY MORNING TO-DO LIST

Based on what I have learned, thought about, underlined, and highlighted, here is my list of things I want to do first thing "Monday morning" ….

People simply don't make eye contact anymore.
—Eric Kripke

Signals

"Smile and make eye contact"

As amazingly simple as it sounds, smiling and making eye contact is among the best networking secrets. You learned this one at about age 2. Seriously.

Have you ever tried to have a conversation with a person who is scowling, looking aloof, or not even looking at you? It really doesn't work well at all.

Gazing, staring, looking comatose

Ultimately, there is a fine line between staring and making eye contact. People are also fairly adept at figuring out if you are looking them in the eyes, or if you are staring at something or someone else.

Be aware of cultural differences – in some parts of the world, looking into someone's eyes, especially for more than a brief glance, is considered rude.

To be successful at networking, you'll need to figure out the differences and nuances, and make sure that you adapt to each situation.

Be in the moment

• Introduce yourself, clearly stating your name, and then repeat their name to make sure you got it right.

• Resist the temptation to "scan the room" looking for someone better while having conversations.

• Maintain good eye contact without staring.

• Smile enough to convey friendliness but not so much as to appear deranged.

The handshake alert

Your handshake may be the only physical contact that you have with the other person. Research shows that it definitely creates a specific impression in the other person, whether it is subtle or not.

To stack the odds for your success, you want to go for a firm and confident handshake.

Period.

If you do any amount of networking, you'll discover that quite a few wacko handshakes exist. Make no mistake about it, wacko doesn't inspire confidence. Wacko simply makes someone uneasy, often on a subconscious level.

Let me again repeat, go for a firm and confident handshake.

Don't overthink it. Don't over analyze it. It is that simple.

Since we've all experienced these wacko handshakes at some point, following are some useful pointers.

AVOID using handshakes that incorporate any of the following issues:

• Squeezing the other person's hand very hard.

• Mashing the other person's fingers in a vice-like grip.

• Hooking into the other person's skin with fingernails.

• "Serial-killer dominant twist" where you try to twist the other person's hand so your hand ends up over their hand (by the way, rather than proving your supposed superiority, this style only demonstrates that you have a super weird and pretentious handshake).

• Limp/lifelessness.

• Sticky or moist skin (at events, hold your drink/glass in the hand you DON'T shake with to avoid the cold/wet hand syndrome).

• Awkwardly prolonged beyond-several-actual shakes.

• Extending your hand too far or not enough.

• Putting out your hand directly after sneezing or coughing into it, or right after touching your nose or digging in your teeth.

• Placing your hand into another's as if you are the Queen of England, often with no shake attempt.

• Any other clever versions that make people queasy.

If you are on the receiving end of any of these shakes, then consider yourself lucky as you have learned volumes about the other person in mere seconds…

> ***Physical fitness is not only one of the most important keys to a healthy body, it is the basis of dynamic and creative intellectual activity.***
> —John F. Kennedy

Staying Healthy

Quite a few of the professionals I've trained complained to me that they seemed to always be getting sick from all of the networking events they attended. Sniffles, coughs, sore throats, colds, and sometimes worse.

Not too long ago, if you kept washing your hands for fear of germs, you were regarded as a nut. The old TV series, the Odd Couple, depicted an over-the-top germaphobe, Felix Unger. Well, "over-the-top" for those days. Now, he might have been cutting edge…

Fast forward to a few years ago when the US Centers for Disease Control and Prevention (CDC) as well as a host of other agencies including the Mayo Clinic and the World Health Organization (WHO) were all trumpeting the use of hand sanitizers to stop the spread of nasty diseases.

Hand sanitizers have mushroomed all over the place, from office buildings to waiting room to schools to rest rooms. How times have changed. And now, some scientists fear we are contributing to the possible emergence of "super germs" with all the sanitizing we're doing. You just can't please everyone.

Quite a few professionals have wondered out loud in training sessions: *maybe I can get away with not shaking hands?* which is a perfect lead in to my following thoughts.

Years ago, I did work for a client who pretty much refused to shake anyone's hand. (Still doesn't.) He was adamant that most people had atrocious personal hygiene habits, and were sick half the time. Also, he was convinced that it was more than likely that anyone he met had not washed their hands after using the facilities.

My awareness now raised, I, too, started witnessing countless people not washing their hands, and I tried my best to graciously avoid handshaking. I didn't make it a day before I had no choice but to shake…

The deciding factor was that my client was a billionaire and able to get away with it. The rest of us are pretty much stuck with the handshake… germ party and all.

Having served for many years as a N.Y.S. Fire Police Lieutenant responding to a wide variety of scenes that were medically dangerous and potentially infectious, I had been trained to avoid trouble. Yet I honestly hesitated to include this section at all, at the risk of sounding over the top.

Oh, and to satisfy my attorney, I must state that I am *not* a doctor – so if you need medical advice seek that same from a competent professional…

Here are the two things that work for *me*:

> 1) It turns out that good old Mom was right when she insisted on you washing your hands frequently.

2) Don't touch your face (especially not your eyes, ears, nose, or mouth) after being in contact with and *shaking hands* with other people. You will be providing potential fast entry into your system to any germs that might have gotten on your hands. Wash those hands first (see #1).

The reason I devoted a lot of ink to this topic is purely selfish – on *your* behalf! If you go to loads of networking events, you are that much more exposed to germs. And when you get sick, you aren't able to network effectively, if at all. You're out of commission – literally. You only get networking results when you're networking.

So, if you can't physically wash your hands, don't forget your hand sanitizer. Use it discreetly, as necessary, but definitely sanitize upon exiting an event. Better safe than sorry.

ACTION STEPS

• Practice introducing yourself. A mirror works well. You might as well see what the other person will be seeing.

• Make a concerted effort to listen intently to the person with whom you are chatting for the entire time you're chatting.

• Assess your handshake and make necessary modifications, as appropriate.

MONDAY MORNING TO-DO LIST

Based on what I have learned, thought about, underlined, and highlighted, here is my list of things I want to do first thing "Monday morning" ….

_____
_____
_____
_____
_____
_____
_____
_____
_____
_____
_____
_____
_____
_____
_____
_____
_____
_____
_____
_____
_____
_____

> *The joy of life comes from our encounters with new experiences, and hence there is no greater joy than to have an endlessly changing horizon, for each day to have a new and different sun.*
> —Christopher McCandless

Unclumping

"Don't clump"

We've all done it. We get to a networking event, find a buddy, and "clump." And sometimes, even more buddies join us as the clump grows and grows…

But this defeats the purpose of going to a networking event in the first place.

Most professionals don't have loads of free time to begin with, so use your networking time judiciously. While it is great to connect with all of your "buddies," make sure that you "unclump" at events, and discover new people.

EXPANDING YOUR REACH

Networking is as much about building and strengthening your existing relationships as it is about expanding your reach into new groups.

So, while it is important to meet up with and reconnect with familiar faces, it is just as important to make contact with people you don't yet know.

A MATTER OF BEING SEEN

Strengthening existing relationships is often as simple as being seen. People are so overwhelmed with messaging and data that it is not uncommon for them to forget loads of things, including you and your services. The simple act of seeing you or bumping into you can often jog their memory and bring you back into the fold.

Networking also raises your profile. It gets you noticed. Being seen amongst movers and shakers can rub off in a good way. Conversely, hanging out with a lackluster crowd can drag you down. Seek out the stars and shine bright.

EXPANDING BY DOING

Expanding your reach is often as simple as mingling and interacting with new groups of people whenever and wherever you get the chance.

The disconnect happens when you stop or give up since you haven't achieved instantaneous results. This is often based on a belief that you should be getting back enormous results every time you network.

Well, I'm here to tell you that networking is often like prospecting for minerals – sometimes you'll work at it for days and weeks and find little, if anything. And sometimes you'll hit a mother lode after a few whacks of your networking hammer.

The only thing I can promise you without a shadow of a doubt is that if you do nothing, you'll strike nothing – every time. You really do have to be out there in order to reap the rewards.

"ATTENDANCE DYNAMICS" MAGIC

The first time you show up at an event or meeting, you're often seen as a newcomer, an outsider, a veritable fly-by-night-er.

The second time, you're a repeat offender.

By the third or fourth time, you may find that you've been magically transformed into a "regular."

And with your new "regular" status, other "regular" attendees will suddenly pay more attention to you.

Time and time again, I have seen other regulars open up only after a newer member had participated regularly for some time. It's almost as if they're waiting to see if you'll last. Then suddenly, once you're accepted as a regular, you are brought into conversations and dealings at a much higher level.

I am all for pulling the plug before wasting loads of time and resources, but attendance dynamics is one strong reason why it often pays to give a regularly scheduled networking group or networking meeting more than only one try.

ACTION STEPS

• Make a commitment NOT to clump.

• Look for ways to branch out and expand your circle.

• Use the power of Attendance Dynamics to boost your acceptance and credibility.

Unity is strength... when there is teamwork and collaboration, wonderful things can be achieved.
—Mattie Stepanek

Teamwork & the Power of the Third Party Endorsement

Ever go to an event only to meet someone who is very impressed with ... themselves?

They go on and on about how great they are. *Yawn.* And just when you think they are finished, they turn to you and say, "Oh, enough about me talking about me. Let's find out what you think about me."

Painful.

But here is the conundrum.

You want to say great stuff about yourself to catch the attention of prospective clients. You want to throw in all those things you know you are so great at.

But then you worry that if you boast about yourself, then you will sound, well, like a complete jerk. So, do you get overly modest and down play stuff? Not very effective.

What to do?

Over the course of many years of trial and error, I discovered a very effective strategy to overcome this hurdle. One word. Teamwork. Team up with someone so both of you can then "work" the room together.

Here is how it works. You and I team up and attend a networking event with one another. We walk the room and approach people as a team and speak to them together.

One hand washes the other

In a very brief and conversational manner, I introduce you as a consummate professional, mention your top areas of expertise, your main service offerings, and end with several very successful outcomes you've had for thrilled clients. I then turn it over to you as I say something along the lines of, "Well, I think I got that right but is there anything I missed?" You thank me and proceed to add a little more color as you build your brand image. Then we turn to the other person and ask them about themselves. Once they are done, you turn to me and introduce me as I just did for you.

Once the intros are over, and during the regular conversation, we continue to help each other. For instance, after you mention a new service you are offering, I can chime in and add something relevant, such as how that service benefitted someone I know, et cetera. Then you make a comment that leads into what I do and after I tell a short story about what I do and how it has helped a client, you jump in and vouch for me and my services.

Water ballet

Great care must be taken not to sound rehearsed or to fawn. Keep it real and natural. Stay true and honest. Yet don't forget to sell me a little as I will sell you. It takes practice, but when it works, it's like water ballet.

You cannot imagine how highly effective this approach can be, especially when you are virtually unknown to the prospective client or referral source.

Harnessing the power of third party endorsements

Let's chat a moment about exactly why this approach can be very powerful. The secret lies in the power of "third party endorsements." It's when someone else vouches for someone or something.

You know, I tell you why I prefer BMW, you tell me why Montblanc pens are the best, John tells us to try Del Frisco's, Sally swears by Harman Kardon. We each back up our views with personal anecdotes and experiences. And you listen, taking it all in.

We might also perceive media reports, news stories, newspaper or magazine articles, and other such content as unbiased endorsements as well. Again you listen, taking it all in.

And because you and I see the "endorser" as an unbiased source, we give more credence to what they are saying as opposed to what we see as biased testimonials – commercials, ads, advertorials, paid celebrity endorsements, email blasts, infomercials, someone talking about themselves, et cetera.

Wait a minute. What did you say in that last part of your last sentence?

Are you saying that someone talking about themselves isn't credible?

No. Not necessarily. It depends on how they do it.

If someone comes up to you and announces that they are a "genius," you think: *what an egotistical jerk*. Yet, if someone else points them out and tells you that that person is a "genius," suddenly you are more likely to consider it.

Many of us are preconditioned to be on guard and somewhat skeptical when we hear someone detailing their own accomplishments.

If they drone on too much, or seem too impressed with themselves and their mighty abilities, or make short stories long, you might find yourself starting to wonder just how "real" they are. At a minimum, you might find yourself thinking how vain or conceited the person is. Or, you may dismiss them altogether as complete braggarts and egoists. Or worse.

Ok, I can see that, so what do I do when I am alone and must do my own introduction?

I would stick with some version of the formula: "You know how…….well I help……my clients tell me that they value….."

We will cover this approach later during the "Elevator Speech" discussion. Be on the look-out for it.

So going to networking events with a teammate really has a lot of advantages. Instead of me trying to impress another person with "me," my teammate does it for me.

Exactly. And then you do the same for them.

Any other pointers?

Yes. Read on.

> *Sincerity makes the very least person to be of more value than the most talented hypocrite.*
> —Charles Spurgeon

Sincere & Natural Wins the Day

There are some very specific caveats, warnings, and "Dos and Don'ts" that I get into during my consulting sessions and training seminars.

These include:

- how to approach prospects.
- how NOT to sound "scripted."
- the three things that will positively sink this technique faster than you can say "NOTworking."
- how to choose the perfect partner, and
- the ONE thing you must NEVER EVER overlook.

But, in this book, let's realize that you must strive to be as "sincere" and as "natural" as you possibly can for maximum results.

Nothing can trump being honest and straightforward.

Know *before* you go

It is also highly suggested that you and your "networking team" partner set some goals and ground rules BEFORE you venture out into the crowd.

DON'T just simply get together, exchange some vague points about each other, and then "venture out" into the great unknown. At a minimum, I would suggest that you make sure you each understand, in at least a basic way, what each of you is looking to *offer* to a client, and what each of you is looking for *in* a client.

Commit to getting it right

Rehearse your introductions with each other *in person* a few times at least. Correct each other. This is NOT the time to be shy.

You definitely don't want your first time hearing their attempt at introducing you to potential clients to be at an event where it is far harder to make corrections. Remember, you are going for "sincere and natural."

By the way, live corrections can be problematic. A few little snafus are fine. Make some polite corrections and move on. It happens to the best of us. But if it starts to sound like you folks don't really know each other all that well, then you risk losing any value that your purported third party endorsement might have conveyed.

So back to "knowing before going" – make sure your networking partner is introducing you exactly the way you want to be introduced – that your main points and service offerings are covered, and that there is at least one compelling client success story to end with. And vice-versa.

Detail is NOT king

To be effective, your partner doesn't need to know every nuance and every detail about your offerings or success stories. She or he just has to say enough to tee you up – to give you the platform from which you can take over the microphone and continue…

It is an evolving effort

Professionals often decide to specialize, or they may completely change direction. Some service offerings evolve, others atrophy. At times, firms may launch new departments, or choose to cease various efforts. Firms merge and sell out. Laws and regulations change. Sometimes, the market lustily seeks certain services while growing tired of others.

So it is important to take this naturally evolving landscape into consideration when you prep for events.

Even if your space is relatively even-keeled, you and your teammate will likely want to highlight different points at different events at different times of the year. New service offerings, current successes, and even trending or seasonal offerings might be top of mind.

Thus, it is essential to always try and touch base before every networking event, even after you have gained a mutual comfort level. A simple "anything new I should or shouldn't mention" call or email can work wonders.

In the meanwhile, nothing beats practice.

Practice does not make perfect.
Only perfect practice makes perfect.
—Vince Lombardi

Practice, Practice, Practice

As with any effort, the longer you team up with the same person, and the more you do events together, the better and more effective you will become at intros, and vouching for each other. You will gain a trust in each other's abilities to interact effectively and will be looking out for each other's mutual interests.

This is covered in great detail during my hands-on sessions, but suffice it to say that you want to be as sure as possible that each of you can introduce each other in a compelling way that leads people to want to hear more, rather than roll their eyes or tune out.

Practice, practice, practice.

Did I mention practice?

I get it. I get it. But I'm not sure how an interchange would sound in real-life?

Maybe the following real-life example will help illustrate the point.

Pretend you are at a networking event with me. You're a successful entrepreneur.

Someone has just introduced a professional to you.

Take a moment and compare these two introductions:

"I would like to introduce my friend Jen to you. She specializes in working with clients to make sure that you keep as much cash each year as you possibly can, allowing you to build and accumulate wealth, rather than having to make it over and over and over again. As a tax attorney, she also makes it her business to know the ins and outs of the latest regulations and how you can take advantage of them. Believe me, not everyone knows this stuff like Jen. In fact she recently saved one client over a half million dollars, and that was after their accountant had said he had done all he could. But maybe she should tell you about that. Jen…"

VERSUS

"This is Don the attorney. He works at a large law firm. He does legal work."

Can you guess from these introductions alone which networker commands more interest?

If at first you don't succeed

Not everything works out the way it was planned. People forget or stumble or whatever. Networking teams run hot and cold. But…

If you should find that your networking team partner

- isn't reciprocating properly
- isn't giving you your fair share of limelight

- is happily accepting your introductions of praise and your lofty endorsements but isn't doing the same for you…well..

Maybe they are not "getting it," and a simple conversation to connect the dots will wake them up.

Or maybe they are simply selfish and self-centered. No amount of talking will get them past their inward focus. It's all about them and them alone.

If any of these items are the case, then it is time to move on.

UPGRADE!

Your time as a professional is your most valuable commodity. If you are actively investing your time in networking with a team partner, and that team partner isn't living up to their end of the bargain, then upgrade before your next networking event. Find that networking partner that will complement you as well as you complement them. (complement with an "E" as in match, pair, accompany, balance, et cetera.)

Finding the perfect networking partner

Several decades have proven that there is almost no way to predict who will make the perfect networking teammate for you. It really comes down to a whole bunch of educated guesses and trial and error.

But if I were asked to help stack the odds for your success, here are some of the things I might mention:

Try and pair up with someone from another firm or niche or discipline or practice group.

I have found that one accountant and one lawyer are often a wonderful pairing. Same goes for a lawyer and a financial planner, and a consultant and an accountant. You get the picture.

You can also pair with a professional who is in your same field – however make sure you can articulate what the other does that is unique and special. For example, two accountants could successfully team network if one were, say, a state sales tax expert, and the other specialized in trusts and estates.

The point is, for maximum impact, each of you needs your own domain and specialty area to talk about. And it needs to be different enough so you can shine and not step on the other's toes.

ACTION STEPS

• Try and team up with another person for purposes of working networking events.

• Work the power of the third party endorsement while being sure to stay natural and sincere.

• Plan out your networking activities so that you and your trusted team member are both available and will be able to implement the team approach.

• Rehearse the team approach. Don't be shy about correcting the way you want your team member to introduce you or what the team member should say about you. Make sure to do the same for them. And practice.

• Upgrade till you find a terrific networking partner.

MONDAY MORNING TO-DO LIST

Based on what I have learned, thought about, underlined, and highlighted, here is my list of things I want to do first thing "Monday morning" ….

_____

_____

_____

_____

_____

_____

_____

_____

_____

_____

_____

_____

_____

_____

_____

_____

_____

_____

_____

_____

I remind myself every morning: Nothing I say this day will teach me anything. So if I'm going to learn, I must do it by listening.
—Larry King

Listening

"Listen, really listen"

Have you ever "woken up" half way through a conversation?

Have you ever day-dreamed while "listening" to someone?

Embarrassing, right?

When you are trying to make a good impression, especially at networking events, it really is important to stay focused. Pay attention. Really practice listening. You may be amazed at what you hear.

Pay attention to the conversation

As you converse, nothing screams louder than facial expressions that are inappropriate to the context. Add in some poorly executed gratuitous phrases, such as "great, great" and you have a recipe for disaster.

I was at an event when a particularly self-absorbed networker, "Pompous Dude," was half-listening to someone who suddenly started to talk about how their mother had recently died.

Pompous Dude kept adjusting his tie, grinning ear to ear, and saying, "Great, great. That's just so great."

Clearly, he hadn't been listening one damn bit.

If it was *your* personal story of death, how would you have felt at his idiotic reaction? I mean, really?! It couldn't have been worse and no amount of explanations or clever excuses could ever make up for that lack of sensitivity.

You can rest assured that Pompous Dude didn't make a good impression on anyone.

To this day, people avoid sending him referrals based on that fateful slip, reasoning that he is unpredictable and doesn't pay attention to details. His grin is rather disturbing as well.

Ouch.

Back to listening – really listening. While you are listening, really listening, keep a look out for any connections you can make for the person with whom you are conversing. You needn't feel obligated to give away the ranch, but if in the course of your conversation you see some natural connections, consider making them.

Better yet, make some connections at the event itself. I am known for connecting people at events on the spot simply because I listen, remember various people and what they are looking for/offering, and can process a tremendous amount of data seemingly instantaneously.

On-the-spot-connections trump follow-ups any day.

Playing the FOCUS Game

It is fine to move on, but during the time you are interacting, don't get distracted.

As hard as it might be at first, train yourself to give everyone a good deal of respect and attention, during that bit of your time that you have already committed at networking events.

It may help to play the "Focus Game" where you treat each individual as a test of your focusing skills. Build a "mental screenplay" out of your conversation, linking topics of discussion to the pictures you paint in your mind. Be as vivid as possible, and allow your natural curiosity to create a robust picture.

As you interact, listen for clues to people's needs and think if it makes sense to try and connect them to your sources and contacts.

If you find yourself losing interest, snap yourself back by adding some energy to conversations by asking open-ended questions. Sticking to questions that can't be answered with a *yes* or *no* will help engage both sides.

Just as in court, some great questions can lead to some very telling comments.

It doesn't just have to be "business"

A one-track conversation that focuses solely on business may be appropriate in some situations, but mixing it up a bit often yields better results. Get creative with those open-ended inquiries.

Instead of "How's business?" why not try:

- What is the most interesting question a client has asked you lately?
- What electronic gadget can't you live without?
- What is the most critical issue in your industry today?
- What is your favorite hobby?
- How do you handle difficult clients?
- If you had to do it all over again, what would you do differently, and what would you do the same?
- Where do you see your business in 5 years?
- Where is the most productive place you have found for networking?

Use every answer and new piece of information that you gather to build that mental screenplay of the person you're speaking with. If you do it right, you may be surprised just how much data you remember about them the next time you run into them.

If you lose your focus, don't waste any time getting back on course

Hey, we're all human. Sometimes you'll miss an important point. Maybe you won't hear something correctly. Maybe your mind just wandered for a moment.

Whenever the case once you've realized it, simply ask people to repeat themselves—or even to clarify a point.

Better to ask and get back to the same page, rather than to pretend to be there, or worse yet, to bluff.

ACTION STEPS

• Commit to full attention networking. Make a mental effort to stay engaged.

• *Ask* if you're not sure.

• Focus on people and always be listening for any subtle clues.

• Try your own version of the "Focus Game," rewriting the rules as necessary until it works well for you.

MONDAY MORNING TO-DO LIST

Based on what I have learned, thought about, underlined, and highlighted, here is my list of things I want to do first thing "Monday morning" ….

A wise man can learn more from a foolish question than a fool can learn from a wise answer.
—Bruce Lee

The ONE question you MUST ask

Ask people why they are there – and what they hope to accomplish

Without a doubt, the above question is the most powerful question I have ever used at networking events. It has the potential to get at the heart of "motivation." You may not always get an accurate answer at first, but keep probing in a respectful way with follow up questions to find out the truth behind your new friend's motivation for being at the networking event.

Honest answers

At one event, I turned one of the attendees and asked my famous **"So, why are you here at this event? What are you looking to get out of it?"** The young man smiled, and answered, "My boss made me attend. My goal is to get out of it, you know, leave as soon as possible."

Here are some memorable and not-so-memorable answers I have heard over the years:

- "I am here to find a new accounting firm since my current one missed another deadline, again."

- "My friend asked me to come with her."

- "I have a printing business and I want to find new clients. What does your firm need?"

- "I have a feeling my attorney doesn't know much about trust and estate work, so I need to find someone who does."

- "I am looking to retire, so I am starting to speak to people to see if any wants to buy my practice."

- "My firm sponsored the event, so here I am. Where's the food?"

The minute you have uncovered their true motivation(s), you are on your way to making the most of the situation.

A conversation is a dialogue, **not** *a monologue. That's why there are so few good conversations: due to scarcity, two intelligent talkers seldom meet.*
—Truman Capote

Keep the Conversation Flowing

Experts will tell you that the person who does most of the speaking during a pleasant and productive conversation often leaves thinking that that the *other* person was nice, smart, attentive, and caring. So be sure to *listen more* than you speak.

In the meanwhile, here are some ways to keep a conversation flowing.

- People are often conditioned to give boring, straight, safe answers at first. Probe politely to get closer to the truth.

- Don't assume that the first answer people give is real. Ask follow-up questions to clarify. Don't forget those open-ended questions.

- Don't overdo the questions. You're not a homicide detective. Asking too much, too soon, can turn people off really fast.

- Above all, be genuine, be yourself, have fun, and be fun to be around.

Often, when you make the conversation about *them*, you'll rarely run out of stuff to chat about!

The object of life is not to be on the side of the majority, but to escape finding oneself in the ranks of the insane.
—Marcus Aurelius

Escaping

Sometimes, it is just time to move on. The conversation has reached its logical (or illogical) conclusion. You're getting that distinct "Alrighty then, see ya" feeling. It's just not working. It's no longer productive. It may never ever be productive....Yet the other party is not getting the message. They are just standing there smiling or chatting away or whatever. You have developed a tail, a shadow, a hang around, and you want *out*. While you wish to be polite, you also need to be respectful of your own time – your goal is business development, not psychological analysis.

What do you do?

Many professionals have told me that they politely excuse themselves to go to the restroom. But what if "they" wait for you to return from the restroom?

Of course, you can politely excuse yourself with "So nice to have met you" and try to move on. Or maybe simply comment that the networking event looks like it has tremendous potential and that you are excited to meet some more people, and so should they be equally excited to meet some other new people. Hint. Hint.

So, after multiple trips to the restroom, and all manner of verbal extraction attempts, they are still glued to you. Now what?

One of the best ideas from a master networker was to simply introduce them to another attendee that may be a more appropriate match for them, and then move on, leaving them with their new friend. While this takes a bit of effort on your part, it is non-confrontational and gives off win-win vibes. I actually used this technique to shake off an aggressive networking event "stalker." I connected him to someone who happened to be standing nearby. To this day, he thanks me. Apparently, the two of them embarked on a lucrative business relationship. Who would have guessed?

ACTION STEPS

• At your next networking event, try and find out in a polite way why the person you are speaking with is at the event.

• Politely probe a bit to get to a "new" truth.

• Maintain professionalism and an easy going conversational attitude for maximum impact.

• Don't forget to mention what you bring to the table, as appropriate.

• It doesn't hurt to have an escape plan.

MONDAY MORNING TO-DO LIST

Based on what I have learned, thought about, underlined, and highlighted, here is my list of things I want to do first thing "Monday morning" ….

You don't have to play masculine to be a strong woman.
—Mary Elizabeth Winstead

ONLY* for Women

As a woman at a networking event, you have a variety of advantages. Realize it and go to town!

Listening and caring

First, my observations lead me to believe that women are often better listeners than men.

Instead of jumping in, as males so often do, to immediately "solve problems," women tend to listen more and then ask really good questions.

So as a woman, use your natural talent for listening and interacting to your advantage. While the men run around showing off and blurting out "solutions," show prospective clients that you really understand and actually care about their needs and business challenges. Ask the questions that get to the heart of their concerns and seek to establish deep connections that superficial small talk really won't accomplish.

Gut feelings

Second, I've seen that women have an uncanny intuition about people. If that's you, then use your gift to your advantage at networking events to weed out the drones and concentrate on the more robust prospects. Follow your gut. Build connections and develop relationships at the event by showing people that you are interested in them – ask real questions and focus all your attention on them during your interactions. Go for quality exchanges rather than quantity.

No airs

Third, women will often be able to network more effectively because of their ability to be authentic and natural. At almost any balanced networking event, I've seen more men than women "posturing" and putting on airs. Hiding behind "power ties" and suits "of armor," men seem more likely to exaggerate, while women often seem more genuine. Use your natural personality to make positive memorable impressions while the braggarts and boasters swill around you.

Never let anyone make you feel less than they are

On a final note, let's chat for a moment about chauvinists. I observed an old-timer at an event who was clearly very impressed with himself and his perceived accomplishments as a partner at a larger firm. But instead of inspiring or respecting those around him, he zeroed in on several people and shooed the rest away. Clearly, he was still trying to come to terms with the fact that women won the right to vote. It seemed that the concept of women in the workplace was also paining him to no end.

Although three very important female business leaders were nearby, he wouldn't give them the time of day, making crude and dismissive comments, and talking over them. He even threw in a few off-color comments.

Luckily, the women instantly realized what an oaf he was and, instead of trying to be polite or argumentative, simply moved on (taking with them their business, contacts, and opportunities). As an aside, the boor's firm lost an enormous opportunity that day but he and his partners (who are seemingly supportive of his ways – hey, he's still at the firm) will never know it.

You don't have to listen only for gems like "honey" or "sweetie" or "where is your boss, little lady?" It can be far more subtle than that. So rely on your oaf-dar (yup, radar that locates oafs) and move on when you're not being treated seriously. There are plenty of other opportunities and better people.

Maintain your confidence. Allow no one to chip away at it. Ever. Remember – you have the power.

*And for those men that read this part - man, you guys just don't follow directions, do you?

Without promotion, something terrible happens... nothing!
—P. T. Barnum

Elevator Speeches or Pitches

From the NYC SURVIVAL GUIDE *page 562:*

Q: "What do you call someone who randomly chats it up with strangers on elevators?"
A: "An assault victim."

There may be more advice floating around on the "elevator pitch" or "elevator speech" than elevators in New York City. As a Manhattan native, you quickly learn not to engage strangers on an elevator. But if this poorly named activity refers to succinctly explaining, in a memorable way, what value you or your business or service brings to the table – then here are some essentials to keep in mind.

Frame your introduction in terms of benefits. Express yourself in plain terms and try to zero in on the kind of clients you want. Don't make your audience work hard to decipher what you bring to the table. Don't make your listeners guess whom they might be able to recommend. This is not the time to throw around vague and broad statements. Better to get a smaller number of targeted referrals rather than lots of off-the-mark time wasters (or no referrals at all).

Remember a while back we spoke about the power of "third party endorsements"? And you may have wondered how this would work for an "elevator speech" since *you* are introducing yourself – and you won't have the benefit of a *third* party endorsement? I have found that one of the best ways to give yourself a legitimate "third party endorsement" is to relate what others have said about you in a non-obnoxious way.

For instance, I have heard super networkers give themselves that "outside endorsement" by saying something along the lines of

> "My clients tell me that what they value most about what I bring to the table is …"

Or some version of

> "my client appreciated the results I was able to get for her so much that she immediately referred me to three of her associates…"

Be crisp and professional. Be well versed. You are speaking about what you do. Don't sound tentative or unsure. Don't umm and aww. Be convincing, positive, and confident. And finally, be memorable.

More on being memorable in a moment.

> *Humility is not thinking less of yourself,*
> *it's thinking of yourself less.*
> —C. S. Lewis

DON'T Lead with Your Title or Degree or Professional License

Instead, try something that will actually catch someone's attention in terms of a *benefit for them*, i.e.: "You know how…….well I help……my clients tell me that they value….."

Dopey intro: "I am a CPA, I have an MBA, and an LLM, and I practice accounting."

Stacking the Odds for Success: "You know how the IRS is actively going after people with foreign bank accounts? Foreign property? Foreign life insurance accounts? And you know how even well-meaning people are getting jammed up? Well, I specialize in helping my clients with foreign assets stay far away from any jails or any other bombshells out there, and legally! My clients tell me that they really value my ability to make complex foreign tax matters simple and painless to deal with. They also know in the unlikely case that if the government does come knocking, I'll be there to guide them through."

The Dopey intro is so vanilla that it says very little. I walk away thinking "another accountant." Yet after that last intro, if anyone in my sphere of influence specifically has foreign asset troubles, I am already connecting dots.

Speaking of which, figure out ways to make your intro "limiting enough" to weed out the world while *focusing in on* your ideal new client. Why waste your time wining and dining the wrong prospects? Wouldn't you rather focus your energy on your ideal targets?

Let's look at another set of introductions:

Dopey: "I can service everyone and every company, tiny and huge. I know all industries. I can do it all, including audits and analyses. I help people with their taxes, and to file all forms properly and on time. I do everything our clients need me to do. I am there for my clients doing loads of work for them all the time."

Stacking the Odds for Success: "I specialize in assisting early start ups and entrepreneurs in the software arena. I really like working with video game developers and business software applications. While I work with companies exclusively in the tri-state area, I am also an expert in internet business sales tax issues and keep my clients out of trouble in all 50 states. Although I am rather flexible, my clients fall in the $500,000-$2,000,000 range in annual sales."

See the differences? See how the first intro says almost nothing and probably didn't bring anyone to mind from the prospect or referral arena? And see how the second intro is so specific that it literally points directly at someone you may actually know? At a minimum, the second intro gave you a very detailed look at who that professional is looking to connect with.

This search for what you want is like tracking something that doesn't want to be tracked. It takes time to get a dance right, to create something memorable.
—Fred Astaire

Be memorable

Have you ever gone out to the store only to forget what you needed to pick up by the time you got there? Have you ever walked into a room to get something, only to realize you had no clue what it was? Have you ever made a mental note to yourself to do something (or to never do something again) only to do the exact opposite?

Have you ever been amazed at all the advertising you've been exposed to only to draw a blank when you need to buy a certain product? If only one name jumps out at you at decision time, then you know that brand has made a huge impression on you. It was memorable while all the others weren't.

Networking is identical.

If "they" don't remember you, then all your clever stories and intros and speeches are for naught.

I repeat – if you're not MEMORABLE, if they don't remember you and don't contact you, then everything else was a waste.

How can I be more memorable?

Let's talk branding. Your branding should help make you stand out from the crowd and be more memorable.

First, how are you packaged?

What is your visual or audio image projection? Are you the sharp dressed one with a killer smile and intense gaze? Are you the one with the unique business card and the ability to listen without interrupting? Are you the one with that unforgettable introduction that people remember to this day? Are you the one with the commanding voice and polished look? Or maybe the one with two different cufflinks who handed out some useful leads? Or the one with her firm logo on her watch? Et cetera, et cetera, et cetera.

Using Madison Avenue Branding Tricks and Techniques

"Be Memorable" comes from my time as an executive at a legendary Madison Avenue agency where we had a saying, "It's all worthless if they don't remember." And since being remembered, as in "top of mind" or "mind share," is very important to being in the game, here is what I would ask you to consider: how do *you* package *you*?

Here's a clever trick from Madison Avenue that you might find useful. The more senses you can link into a brand presentation, the better. Think luxury car: new car leather smell, impeccable shine, luxurious feel, and tuned exhaust sound. (Only "taste" is missing, for obvious reasons.)

- SIGHT: Are you well groomed? Clothes neat and clean? Do you dress for success? Everyone could benefit from a quick wardrobe analysis. You need to learn what style works best for you.

- SOUND: You may not be able to do much with your voice pitch, but you can certainly be sure to speak clearly at a pleasant volume.

- SMELL: "Clean" is the best smell in the world. You may have a signature cologne or perfume and that may be part of your branding, but make sure it is subtle. Too much is FAR WORSE than too little. My favorite scent is still pure "clean."

- TOUCH: Are your hands clean and dry? Not too cold? (Hold your ice cold drippy drinks in the hand you don't shake with.) Do you respect the personal space of strangers? Err on the side of formality rather than being all touchy feely, especially with the opposite sex. Refrain from poking, nudging, back-slapping, and the like. It's likely illegal in at least 47 of the 50 states…

Adding the visual with *words*

Can you think of a clever visual to paint into your introduction that will be memorable?

Something along the lines of "Think of me as…." or "I am just like" …. "When you see me say to yourself…."

A very successful networker I know would wear crisp black suits, an official looking lapel pin, and would paint the following visual with his introduction:

"Think of me as your personal CPA Secret Service bodyguard with only one mission in life, to make sure that you are 100% bulletproof – safe and secure from tax grenades, deduction bombs, withholding bullets, and regulatory terrorists. Wherever you want to take your business, I will map it out first and make sure your way is safe. No landmines. No cliffs. You sleep soundly all night because I am up guarding you 24-7."

His story line and his visual picture were reinforced by the way he dressed and the way his voice almost sounded official. Pretty extreme? You bet – and highly memorable!

Put your own mark on you!

With some thought and effort, could you come up with your own version that works for you?

Without being a clown or sounding arrogant or flippant, I bet you could paint quite a memorable picture that will serve you well. Make it something you can live with for a long time since once you gain traction, you'll want to keep driving that image home.

This part is fun, but don't take it lightly. It will require some serious thought on your part – after all, you are branding you.

Work on the best mix of *sight and sound*, keep *smell* clean and subtle, use *touch* appropriately, and you will be well on your way to creating your positive and memorable brand impression.

And, of course, whatever your "hook," make sure you are memorable solely for the right reasons… no wearing lamp shades, no wacko handshakes, no dancing on the ceiling….

I can hear you thinking, *Wow, that's some phenomenal advice, but what if after I do all the right stuff, they don't call or keep in touch? Then what?*

Glad to know that you are getting to the heart of the matter – you are exactly right to ask that question.

Ultimately, no matter how memorable you were, proper *follow-up* stacks the odds for your success.

A few thoughts on *follow-up* coming up...

ACTION STEPS

- Write out a brief intro for your self using the formula "You know how/well I help/my clients value."

    - You know how…………………

    - Well, I help………………………

    - My clients tell me that they value……………………………..

- Write down the key attributes of your dream target client(s).

- Decide how you want to be memorable, how you will position your personal brand, and then do it.

- Revisit, fine-tune, and adjust as necessary.

MONDAY MORNING TO-DO LIST

Based on what I have learned, thought about, underlined, and highlighted, here is my list of things I want to do first thing "Monday morning" ….

_____
_____
_____
_____
_____
_____
_____
_____
_____
_____
_____
_____
_____
_____
_____
_____
_____
_____
_____
_____

> *I can give you a six-word formula for success:*
> *Think things through - then follow through.*
> —Eddie Rickenbacker

Some Thoughts on Following-up more Effectively

All the "memorable" in the world will be useless without actual follow-up.

No joke. EVERYTHING hinges on follow-up.

You come back from your networking event with great intentions. And then life gets in the way. Before you know it, that pile of business cards is long forgotten.

The other parties are in the same boat, so in spite of all the good intentions, people rarely connect effectively.

On the off chance you focus on that pile of collected business cards at a later date, maybe you'll stare at them and realize that much of what you thought you would remember is gone. Maybe you'll pick a card or two and move them closer to the phone. The rest of the cards get swept aside again.

Worse yet, if you are super-efficient and have scanned in your cards or digitized them quickly, well – sounds great – but experience shows that could be even worse!

But how could that be worse?? Well, at least with those cards lying around, they provided a visible reminder that you need to do something. Once cards are scanned and filed, well, exactly what visual clues do you have?

We haven't even touched upon the fact that, as more time goes by, you too are becoming a faded memory in the minds of those you met as well.

Again, follow-up is critical

During our live training, we devote a good deal of time and effort to *follow-up* techniques and disciplines. It is one of our more popular and productive modules since it seems that this is the area that many professionals seek to understand better.

Here are a few key ideas regarding *following-up* taken directly from some of my best training sessions:

- follow-up quickly to increase the odds of being remembered.

- follow-up immediately upon returning to my office, or at the outside, within one business day of the event.

- use email, social media, phone, or mail, but do something sooner rather than later.

- send over a lead, or interesting info, referencing your conversation.

- connect two people from your network that could be a potential win-win for each other.

- figure out a way to touch base with your growing network regularly.

- use the phone instead of email once in a while and gauge the results – they may surprise you.

- sending over an article or report that features your picture helps people visually remember who you are.

These days, I find it tends to take at least several attempts to finally connect to people. So, continue to try and connect, without inundating or smothering your new contact. My friend, a top New York City public relations pro, calls it being "pleasantly persistent."

If no concrete contact has been successful after a month, I tend to back off a bit. No, I don't give up, but I don't want to be seen as a time waster or come off as a self-serving pest. So I will continue revisiting, just at longer intervals.

When I have interns, I always say, 'Handwritten thank-you notes can make a difference.' People remember that – not an e-mail – a handwritten note in an envelope.
—Andre Leon Talley

Handwritten Notes & the Power of Contrast

For many years I have been a strong proponent of contrasts. Here's why – when done properly, it sets you apart, it is memorable, and it works.

When I was at LHSB/Grey Advertising, we created quite a stir when we inserted ads into major magazines upside down.

Following the power of contrast, when everyone else was doing full color ads, we ran a series of black and white ads and made a huge impact.

Then, we got on Saturday Night Live's radar, they spoofed us, and that added huge numbers to our client's brand recognition and standing.

Later, when I was helping to develop what would become a lucrative new practice niche at a leading regional accounting firm, I intentionally used snail mail while everyone was overusing email. They thought I had lost my mind not to jump on the email bandwagon – they scoffed at the custom envelope I had created, complete with a drawing of a snail on a mail truck, celebrating our choice to use "snail mail."

And a funny thing happened – our target audience of New Media entrepreneurs loved it. They embraced it, and started clamoring for it. For years they asked to be included in those "snail mail" mailing campaigns. And at the same time, our niche grew from zero clients to about a hundred in a year and a half.

Wow!

So one of my current suggestions to capitalize on the power of contrast is "handwritten." While everyone is overlooking the power of the hand-written word, use it to your advantage.

And while you're at it ...

Send handwritten notes with REAL, COLORFUL, HAND-AFFIXED STAMPS and make an even bigger impact.

Add more MEMORABILITY by creating a custom stamp – check out a custom stamp provider such as www.stamps.com for ideas. You could use your logo, or even your PHOTO on a legal US stamp right there on the envelope! What a different way for them to remember "which one" you were…

Double wow!

ACTION STEPS

• Follow a strict follow-up procedure after each and every networking event. Make it a habit.

• Order a stack of "nice to meet you" cards, preferably featuring your firm logo. I prefer blank on the inside so that you have the flexibility to use them for many occasions (follow-up, birthdays, saw you in the news, congratulations, thought you might be interested, etc. etc.).

• Set aside a specific time for follow-up calls/emails each and every week so that you don't let too much time lapse between initial meeting and re-connecting.

• Go to events that you actually have an interest in, since you will be more connected, and you'll enjoy them more. Making the whole networking experience enjoyable and fun is important, or you will quickly figure out ways to avoid "being out there."

MONDAY MORNING TO-DO LIST

Based on what I have learned, thought about, underlined, and highlighted, here is my list of things I want to do first thing "Monday morning" ....

Searching is half the fun: life is much more manageable when thought of as a scavenge hunt as opposed to a surprise party.
—Jimmy Buffett

How to Find Places to Network

Here are just a few thoughts from what could be a day-long discussion.

Think of networking in silos based on end results – where you get new business.

DIRECT: prospective clients

For direct networking, look for those events and gatherings that your prospective clients attend. Check out their trade associations, trade journals, regular club meetings, supplier meetings, trade shows. Use the power of the internet as well as printed sources. Scan the local papers and business papers, too. Ask your current clients for ideas and guidance. Here is where it pays to be creative. You want to go where no one like you usually steps foot…

For instance, I guided a client whom I assisted with building their Elder Care Law niche to attend and present at dementia support group meetings. I sent another client who was building a restaurant practice to a vendor meeting on brick ovens from Italy, and then a POS equipment training session.

While you're at the event, I would network, but I wouldn't "sell." Instead, ask participants where you can learn more about their industry. Find out what they think are the top 2 or 3 such venues or associations. Seek out stuff that's off the beaten path. Then go to those events as well. If you're the only professional services provider attending, you've scored big time.

INDIRECT: referral sources, complementary services

Prospects who fall into the referral source silo could be other professionals or gatekeepers who hand out assignments to the professionals that they know and trust. They choose you, but then you pretty much run the engagement.

Prospects in the complementary service silo are those people that bring you in to do a portion of an assignment that they are working on as well. It is sort of direct, it may become direct, but it starts out more indirect since you aren't the lead professional.

Whatever the case, here it pays to circulate where your indirects circulate. Depending upon the kind of professional you are looking to connect with, use the internet and print materials to find and attend the local state society meetings, bar association meetings, insurance clubs, and other business networking events that you think will bring success. I always try to give one shot to any worthy looking networking venue. I wouldn't be influenced unduly by the opinions of others until you've personally vetted the gatherings for yourself. Different days and times often bring different attendees. Of course, don't waste your time when the venue clearly isn't what you need it to be.

A Few Final Hints

Over the course of many years of conducting training and listening to and reviewing feedback, here are some of the additional hints that I would have called "common sense" a while back, but I now highlight:

- Whether or not everyone else is doing it, drinking alcohol, especially to excess, is not a great idea at networking events – staying sober is priority number one.

- Breath mints can save many deals.

- Don't become too familiar too fast.

- Don't chew gum.

- Dress for success, dress your part, dress appropriately for the occasion – this is not the time to look super sexy or over the top suave.

- DON'T spew a steady stream of corporate "dope jargon" such as paradigm shift, change agent, coopetition, mission critical, and a whole host of other such dregs – it only makes you sound pompous instead of authentic.

Ultimately, you are the author of your success.

Learning new techniques and being exposed to new tools is great, but actually APPLYING them appropriately and consistently is essential.

So, take the best of the ideas you are exposed to and pick out and implement what works for you. Start today!

I sincerely hope you enjoyed this book. For more useful information and material on professional services development, join us at www.TotalBrandMarketing.com where professionals and professional services firms find the tools, training, and resources they need to succeed.

To learn more about practice development training for professional services firms and professionals, visit us at www.TotalBrandMarketing.com/training/

There is a reason that football teams practice their plays over and over again. There is a reason that golfers practice their swings time and time again. And there is a similar reason you and your team should be practicing networking, presentations, and a whole variety of other social interactions over and over until you are getting the results you deserve.

From all of us at Total Brand Marketing –

Best wishes for continued success!

Walter

Walter Timoshenko
WT@TotalBrandMarketing.com

TOTAL BRAND MARKETING
339 Hicksville Road Unit #9
Bethpage NY 11714-0009
516.827.5460
www.TotalBrandMarketing.com

PS: If you think you, your group, or your firm could be getting better business development or professional development results, don't hesitate to contact me. I will take the time to speak to you to assess your situation, and to determine if it is something that I can likely assist with. Email or call me today.

PPS: Don't worry – you and the specifics of your situation will be treated confidentially. No embarrassments. You can only win.

PPPS: I am always interested in feedback so I can make content even that more relevant and timely for my loyal readers. Please email me with any suggestions or comments about topics you would like covered or expanded upon. I'll do my best to address popular themes in upcoming releases. Thanks!

RESOURCES

Over the course of many years, I have come across a variety of resources that could be valuable to professionals. Here they are in no particular order. A listing below is NOT an endorsement. You must do your own due diligence and seek the guidance of a professional. Also, these sites were operating when this list was compiled - but since sites do go up, down, or away, please use your own discretion.

ABA American Bar Association
www.americanbar.org
Especially the sections on Professional Responsibility, Lawyer Advertising, and Marketing

AICPA
www.aicpa.org
Marketing and business development data.

David Maister
www.davidmaister.com
David has retired, but this remains my favorite professional services site, period.

Legal Marketing Association
www.legalmarketing.org
You have to be a member, but loads of marketing and business development content here.

Total Brand Marketing for Professionals
www.TotalBrandMarketing.com
Yes, it's my blog, and I am quite opinionated.

Special thanks

If it takes a village to raise a child, then I was raised up by a city. Over the years I have been blessed to have worked with and around some of the greatest minds and talents in business. Some I knew for years, others for mere moments. Yet they all made lasting impressions. They hail from a variety of industries and professions including law, accounting, consulting, advertising, and finance, and they are the living legends that walk amongst us. If we could only be so lucky to have more of them in the biz world.

In *NO* particular order, my sincerest thanks to them for everything they've taught me:

> Terry Bonaccolta, Michael Frankfurt, Rick Kurnit, Dick Eisner, Brian Tracy, Jerry Spiegel, MC Mike, Bob Harrison, Marcia Goldman, David Maister, Bob Schmidt, Maureen Blair, Robert Reiss, Lisa Davis, Bean're, Harold Levine, Brett James, Linda Sama, Bill Sullivan, Joe Giacalone, Charly Weinstein, James Garner, Chris Loiacono, Joan Sinopoli, Ned Rosenthal, Stu Silfen, Steve Wolpow, Gavin McElroy, Steve O., Michael Mulligan, Mr. Singh, Alan Isaacman, Robert J. Ritchie, Lynn Tilton, Henry Ruhnke, Michael Fox, Jill Kaplan, Jack Kennedy, Mikey the Z, and Jack O'Hollaren.

And to the countless others I have no doubt forgotten!

"Making your firm a better place than you found it"

a few words about TotalBrandMarketing's

"BETTER PLACE" Strategic Retreats

tailored especially for key members of Professional Services Firms, Executive Committees, Management, and Boards.

> "I thought (your conference) was the best I have ever attended…"

> "…it was one of the best if not THE best marketing sessions we have ever had. Everyone felt they learned something and feel hungry to learn and apply more…"

> "…the Association of the Bar of the City of New York has been fortunate to have (you) teach …the Association's members…our smaller firms received advice that was not only priceless to them but also information that never would have been available to them without these … sessions…"

> "Real pleasure…Thank you for all your help and guidance that you have provided…"

If you've ever taken any of my training classes or attended any of my seminars, one of my top themes has always been to "leave your firm a better place."

Although this simple phrase is easy to understand on a surface level, it literally has volumes and layers of benefits that may not be so apparent. While I am often asked to expand on the topic – which I gladly do during my tailored two-day retreats, here are a few words that will hopefully pique your interest.

"Leaving the firm a better place" is an all-encompassing mantra. It is a mindset. It is a program for development. It is a way to gage what you do and what you spend your time on in relation to the good of your firm, now and in the future. It may be a subtle goal at first. It may be over-simplified or under-simplified. And it may be simply misunderstood and misinterpreted. But over time, as its essence becomes ingrained in everybody and everything, it can have some very powerful consequences.

All of a sudden, everyone at the firm has a piece in the success and growth of your firm.

Everyone understands their roles at their levels. The class structure remains while the barriers – them and us – are removed and replaced with an all-encompassing goal.

While space constraints won't permit me to expand upon the many steps and practices involved, correct implementation of the "leaving your firm a better place than you found it" program will lead to:

• more people at more levels joining in on the development of your firm
• less confusion about what needs to be done
• abundant transparency

- more involvement in revenue growth activities
- a higher level of collaboration
- an increase in opportunity sightings
- a growth in team efforts and a decrease in lone-wolf straying
- better understanding and human relations
- increased customer service marks
- greater understanding of the power of personal branding

The wonderful aspect of the program is that it works equally as well for solos and smaller firms as it does for larger departments and organizations.

In a simple way, asking yourself "Am I leaving the firm a better place than I found it?" has a profound effect on your thought process. You may find yourself starting to see the ramifications of everything you do. Or don't do. That's when it gets really interesting. Actually paying attention to what potentially happens to your brand when you don't meet a deadline, deliver on a promise, or properly service a client is not only instructive, it can be very motivating. It may give you that extra push you need, when you've burnt both your candle ends, to go that extra mile.

During new employee orientations, the "leaving the firm a better place" messaging is so much more inspiring than "we strive to provide our clients the best service in the world."

As far as the specifics go, you are simply framing everything you think and do on behalf of your practice and firm in terms of "Are you leaving your firm a better place than you found it?" While it may seem unusual at first, it quickly becomes a habit, providing guidance and a nimble ability to more rapidly decide where to devote your efforts.

When participating in the "Are you leaving your firm a better place than you found it?" program, you will learn to

- be able to quickly say "yes" or "no" to requests for your time
- refer and give out referrals far more effectively
- make the most out of networking events
- create deeper inroads with contacts
- capitalize on organization memberships
- build and grow trust amongst your contacts and especially your clients
- bill far more efficiently and effectively
- manage the work of others with a lot less pain
- shift the emphasis from small and limited goals to the big picture
- hold everyone accountable starting with yourself

And that's just on Day One…

On Day Two of this comprehensive program, you will learn to put everything together for yourself, at your firm, for your department, or wherever you want to implement growth and development. You'll also learn the secrets to shedding the many anchors that will invariably try to stagnate your efforts, or even drag you down. These anchors often include environments, resources, and people – and each element is fully addressed.

WARNING: This is NOT a "fix everything in a day" program. There are plenty of consultants running around hawking those kinds of wild claims. And if you don't intend to actively participate, walk the walk, talk the talk, et cetera, then this program is probably NOT for you.

It is NOT suitable for groups or firms where the leadership hires us to implement the program, then won't support it. Or will only support it in words but not deeds. Save your money. This is an ALL-IN program with plenty of follow-up and commitment. Period.

I know this may come off as somewhat harsh, but believe me when I say that without support and follow-up at all levels, especially the very top, any program is doomed. These days, nobody has time to waste. However, since you've read this far, you are most likely exactly the kind of professional who will best understand what I am saying. You'll even value the fact that I try hard to separate the "casual wishers" from those that are ready and committed to making profound and lasting changes to their organization. And you will excel at living the message.

The secret is FOLLOW-UP

The secret to success with any program is very simple, but it's often the hardest part to accomplish – pure and simple it is "follow-up." And lots of it.

Think back at all of the great concepts and ideas that you have come across in your career. How many did you follow-up on? How many times did you attend seminars and retreats, got all excited and motivated, and as you settled back into your daily routines, your drive and your resolve to "change the world" started to fade until it was less than a whisper? Frankly, it happens to most of us, most of the time. By the way, that's why so many consultants run around selling an endless supply of "training" – few, if any attendees, actually *follow through*.

Just look at all the binders and handouts you've collected over the years. Most people rarely ever refer back. So, baked right into our program is *mandatory* professionally facilitated follow-up that takes place over the course of one year – extendable for additional time-frames, as necessary.

Let's agree that it takes about a month or so to change a habit. Using this metric, our program has incorporated a follow-up program that is designed to frontload the creation of new habits and then to spread out those new understandings across an entire year. Now that's empowering.

If you are interested in more details, feel free to visit our website at www.TotalBrandMarketing.com (while you are there, be sure to sign up for our free newsletter), or contact us by email at info@TotalBrandMarketing.com.

In the meanwhile, ask yourself, "What did I do *today* to leave my firm a better place?"

The answer will be very telling.

Some additional valuable excerpts especially for professionals to peruse

An excerpt from the book

**OFFICIAL BUSINESS DEVELOPMENT SERIES
for Professionals**

How to Make Your Firm a Better Place Than You Found It

But I'm too busy to market....

A common feeling that professionals have about "marketing" is that somehow it encroaches on their "serious" time. It is seen as an annoyance and even a disruption to getting billable work done.

If you see "marketing" as an unrelated task for which you need to stop your world to plow through… then yes, marketing is all the bad things you've thought it to be. But it is so, because of the way you have decided to approach it, define it, and execute it.

When done right, marketing actually becomes second nature and melds seamlessly into daily activities. It takes almost no extra effort and causes no grand disruptions.

For instance, if you train yourself to spend the first 10 - 15 minutes of every day sending cards or notes or information to the people you met or socialized with the day before, then marketing hasn't been annoying. If you set aside some time at the end of each day to scan publications of interest to your clients for timely info that they would be interested in, then marketing hasn't disrupted anything. It could actually be a welcome break from the mundane.

Some additional low stress marketing activities to work in around your "too busy to market" schedule include:

- sending a thank-you card to a referral source

- inviting a prospect out to a mutually interesting business event

- listening to what your clients and contacts are complaining about – there may be gold there

- calling people on their birthdays

- scanning a trade magazine or the internet to pick up a sense of timely issues before seeing a client or prospect in that industry

Over the years, it turned out that many of the professionals who swore to me that they were the "exception" – that they "really were too busy," simply detested business development and preferred to do other things.

It's probably more about how you approach marketing and what you actually do, than the tasks themselves that cause angst.

It really is your mindset that rules.

An excerpt from the book

OFFICIAL BUSINESS DEVELOPMENT SERIES
for Professionals

Presentation Success
Including Hollywood Presentation Secrets

The read-through

Stroke of genius: the morning of the presentation is not the time to dole out roles.

So you've put together your presentation that you feel is your best shot a wooing the prospect. It is professional, neat, error-free and reflects well on you and your firm. Great, but now it is time to carefully choose who will present what parts.

- Who will go over the firm history, resources, and stats?
- Who will introduce the team members?
- Who has the credibility with the prospect?
- Who will do the proposed solution part?
- Who will field fee and pricing questions?
- What about the wrap-up?
- Who will set expectations and outline the next steps?

The importance of a thorough read-through

Get all the team members on the same page by doing a thorough read-through of the presentation. A read-through yields many benefits including the ability to test-drive sound and meaning, actors, voices, pronunciations, the completeness of the script, and more.

How it *really* sounds...

It is absolutely amazing how different words can "sound" when they are spoken, not silently read. What you thought was prose worthy of Shakespeare while in print suddenly sounds like complete dry dribble during your read-through.

Speaking the presentation affords you the luxury of true emphasis, innuendo, and loads of passion with which written word just can't compete. A read-through will allow you to gage if what you thought you were conveying in writing is actually being conveyed when spoken.

Let's not forget the entertainment aspect of any presentation. Since many of us professionals learned to write in a very dry and factual style, a read-through will serve to identify those areas that may need an injection of life. Yes, yes, I agree that you need to convey professionalism... but you don't have to be boring!

Are the presenters you've chosen delivering?

Having everyone in one room read through the presentation will also allow you to critique the performance (or lack thereof) of your prospective presenters. Now is the time to encourage, coach, or replace presenters. If during the read-through a critical team member turns out to be a terrible presenter but needs to be at the presentation no matter what, then at least you know what you are up against *now*, and can whittle their "on-screen" time down as much as possible.

Oh, and picking a great team isn't enough. Remember the two pros from the introduction that blew their big opportunity? There is a lot more to presenting than showing up. Rehearse, rehearse, and rehearse.

Setting the stage for rehearsing

Great Hollywood directors have been known to begin rehearsals by painting a picture of the scene, reminding the actors and extras of the context of the scene, the historical setting, what has happened to other characters just prior to the scene, and asking for the emotions that they are looking for. Similarly, don't overlook the opportunity to start your rehearsal by stacking the odds for success.

Always open with an overview. Paint the big picture for your team. Then make it clear what their *individual* roles will mean to the effort. Be sure to cover the following:

- What will the presentation cover?
- What form will it take (audiovisual, collateral)?
- How much time has been allocated?
- Where will it be held?
- Who will the audience likely be?
- What concerns might the perspective client have?
- What questions are they likely to ask?
- What's the goal of the presentation?
- What do you want to walk away with?

Add anything that might better prepare those who are rehearsing to shine and excel.

How much should be memorized?

Memorizing exact paragraphs is not recommended. Then again, ad-libbing can be as good as it can be bad. Without a teleprompter, even the president of the United States can be at a loss for words. But make sure everyone is clear on their own main points. It is often good to memorize key concepts and work around them with your own words.

Make sure that each presenter understands their individual role as well as how they fit into the whole presentation. This is especially important in case someone forgets a key point. When everybody understands the main goal, any of the presenters can add in a forgotten point or even pick up on it later so that it is not lost.

Rehearsals

Several full length rehearsals should be done to iron out all the glitches, transitions, and flow. Since the presentation should tell a story from beginning to end and come to a logical and satisfying conclusion, it is important not to have cliffhangers – no *first part* of a trilogy. Instead of ending on a confusing or murky note, that lends itself to misinterpretation, you want to wrap up with all the good guys triumphing over the bad guys. The hero's brilliance and aptitude saves the day!

Once you think that your presentation is smooth and pretty close to a final cut, it's time for a *private screening*. Do this next part right and you will be able to stack the odds for your success by gauging audience reaction and comprehension way in advance of the actual presentation date.

About the author

Walter Timoshenko provides brand, management, marketing, and communications training and guidance for professional services firms, businesses, corporations, and NFPs. He specializes in assisting Partners, Managing Members, MPs, Executive Committees, CEOs, Niche Leaders, and other Executives at professional services firms align their marketing, management, and communications strategies for success.

Named by Accounting Today as one of the "Top 100 Most Influential People," Walter created and served as the first Chairman of the AICPA's *Accounting Firm Marketing Forum* held annually in New York City. He also delivers speeches and presentations on marketing, branding, and communications across the country, and was featured at the AICPA's *Future of Accounting Leadership Forum*. As an associate member of the American Bar Association, Walter helped launch one of the earliest series for legal marketing seminars, and frequently taught CLE related courses at the Association of the Bar of the City of New York, as well as at various law schools.

A regular contributor to the professional services marketing and branding site www.TotalBrandMarketing.com, Walter wrote the foreword for "The 7 Secrets of Extraordinary Investors" by Grammy-Award winner William G. Hammer, Jr., and edited a variety of technical books on financing and legal defense. A long-time member of Mensa and *Beta Gamma Sigma*, he was named the first *Henry O. Ruhnke Executive of the Year* for his dedication to the *Executive in Residence Program* at the Tobin College of Business.

A personal thank you!

Thank you for taking your time to purchase and read this Networking Success guide! I hope that it serves you well and helps you get more success out of your professional networking activities.

Effective networking is not always as easy as it may seem. It involves many specific techniques, smart strategies, and sometimes even some luck. Over the years, I personally invested an immense amount of time and quite a lot of money to learn what I presented to you in this book. The road wasn't easy and with this simple guide, I really do hope you will be able to save time, money, and especially avoid the mistakes.

If you feel strongly that this guide has helped you with your networking efforts, I would be sincerely grateful if you would post a short review on Amazon and recommend this guide to others who would benefit..

Also, please visit my blog at www.TotalBrandMarketing.com and sign up for our free newsletter. I'm sure you will find it helpful.

If you have any questions, comments, suggestions, or ideas about this guide, please email me at WT@TotalBrandMarketing.com

Thanks again and have a terrific day!

Walter

How would you like to learn, in less than 10 minutes, how to instantly increase the power of just one of your marketing ideas up to 12X by harnessing the power of "*Power Spin-Offs!*"?

Since this free report offer may be withdrawn or modified at any time,
go NOW to

www.TotalBrandMarketing.com

to subscribe to our FREE newsletter and claim your FREE report.

total brand marketing

Manufactured by Amazon.ca
Bolton, ON